Honour Earth Mother

Basil H. Johnston

UNIVERSITY OF NEBRASKA PRESS
LINCOLN

☺

First Nebraska paperback printing: 2004

Illustrations: Polly Keeshig-Tobias

Library of Congress Cataloging-in-Publication Data
Johnston, Basil.
Honour Earth Mother / Basil H. Johnston ; [illustrations, Polly
Keeshig-Tobias].—1st Nebraska pbk. printing.
P. CM.
ISBN 0-8032-7622-2 (PBK.: ALK. PAPER)
1. Ojibwa Indians. 2. Ojibwa philosophy. 3. Ojibwa Indians—Religion.
4. Indigenous peoples—Ecology. I. Title.
E99.C6J62 2004
299.7'83330212—DC22   2004004310

Honour Earth Mother

CONTENTS

INTRODUCTION

*"To you Kitchi-Manitou has given the Book.
To us He has given the Earth."*

≈

RED JACKET OF THE SENECA NATION

In 1805 a delegation of West European missionaries came to the Six Nations in Upper New York State to invite them to accept Christianity and civilization. The Six Nations peoples listened to the overture, then retired apart with their orator to consider the missionaries' invitation and to discuss what reply they ought to give the bearers of the "Good News."

Red Jacket, the celebrated orator of the Seneca Nation, gave the reply on behalf of the Six Nations there gathered. It was a classic answer. In declining the invitation to become Christian and civilized, Red Jacket told the missionaries "To you the Great Spirit has given the book, to us He has given the earth."

Learning comes not only from books but from the earth and our surroundings as well. Indeed, learning from the mountains, valleys, forest and meadows anteceded book knowledge. What our people know about life and living, good and evil, laws and the purposes of insects, birds, animals and fish comes from the earth, the weather, the seasons, the plants and the other beings. The earth is our book; the days its pages; the seasons, paragraphs; the years, chapters. The earth is a book, alive with events that occur over and over for our benefit. Mother Earth has formed our beliefs, attitudes, insights, outlooks, values and institutions.

We owe the earth our all, more than we can take in, more than we can say. We can never return anything but our respect and thanksgiving.

In offering a whiff of incense in the Sacred Pipe ceremony to Mother Earth we acknowledge that.

When we hunger, Mother Earth nourishes us. Whatever we need is there in abundance, more than enough to fill the wants and needs of every insect, bird, animal, fish, man and woman with fruit, vegetables, seeds and nectars.

When we need to clothe our bodies from the sun, wind, rain, snow and insects, Mother Earth provides the means to cover our bodies. She gives fat and pelt to the deer, beaver, moose, buffalo, rabbit and bear. They, our older brothers and sisters, lend us their coats. To care for ourselves, our families and our communities, Mother Earth yields the means by which we make our weapons, canoes, snowshoes, clothing, utensils, adornments, and our homes.

When we need shelter from the winds, snows, storms, rains, cold and heat, there are woods, forest, valleys, mountains, bays, and inlets where insects, birds, animals and humans may find harbour, build their nests and dens, or erect their dwellings and found their villages and towns.

When we are sick and need care to nurse us back to health, Mother Earth's meadows, forests, and shorelines are lush with berries, plants, roots, seeds and resins that bear the elixir of health and life. Our ancestors called medicine "Mashki-aki", the strength of the earth for its capacity to infuse the enfeebled sick with energy and vitality.

When our spirits flag and are burdened with cares, worries, losses and sorrows, Mother Earth comforts us. She whispers and chants to the downhearted and dispirited through the tree tops, over the meadows, in cascades and rapids. It is a mother's soothing voice offering solace to the low in spirit. She whispers, "I love you. I care."

And who can be so fair? In the morning light and at sunset,

Mother Earth sparkles. In the spring she glows, and in the autumn she radiates, content that she has provided well for her children. Mother Earth is beauty and goodness.

Our ancestors learned what they knew directly from the plants, insects, birds, animals, the daily changes in the weather, the motion of the wind and the waters, and the complexion of the stars, the moon and the sun. They didn't write these down but kept them in their hearts.

They asked questions. Where did I come from? What am I doing here? Where am I going? Why does life end? Their minds gave them answers to these age-old, world-wide questions. There must be a Creator, Kitchi-Manitou, a mystery, The Great Mystery that brought everything into being. For no man or woman could do what was done, bring into being mountains, plains, forests, lightnings, thunders, rains, change the seasons, light the sun, the moon and the stars and the northern lights; yes, no one but an Unknown Being.

From their observations, our ancestors saw a kinship between plants, insects, birds, animals, fish and human beings, a kinship of dependence; humans depending on animals and birds and insects; animals depending on insects and plants; insects depending on plants; plants depending only on the earth, sun, and rain. Creation was con-ducted in a certain order: plants, insects, birds, animals and human beings. In the order of necessity, humans were the last and the least; they would not last long without the other forms of beings.

Insects, birds and animals do their part in sustaining the act of creation. In the bosom of Mother Earth they bury seeds which become trees, shrubs, plants and flowers. They, and we, take part in creation by re-creating. When living things die, they become part of the earth, a sacred burial ground deserving of reverence. We are the earth, as are eagles, wolves, ants and whitefish.

From seeds come life. From a seed of sound came the stars, the sun, the moon and the earth. The seed rent the silence and the vacuum. After that came other seeds that turned into cedars, sage, sweetgrass and tobacco, sparrows, bears, mosquitoes and spiders, men and women.

When men and women set out on the Path of Life, it was the wolf who felt sorry for the humans and accompanied them and taught them how to hunt, what to eat and what not, where to find food, where to shelter in winter, what deer, beaver, foxes, and mice were like.

Whatever our ancestors needed to know about life and conduct was there performed in the skies, in the trees, on the meadows and in the waters.

The wolf taught the first man and woman about the character, nature and the habits of deer, and what traits the hunter must possess to bring down a deer, a creature wary and faster than the wolf. The wolf does not rush upon its quarry. Instead, it stalks it. Though famished, the wolf shadows the deer, holding its impulses in check. Wolf harries his quarry to anxiety and weakness. Then, when the deer's strength is sapped, the wolf rushes forward and leaps upon its hapless victim. The deer staggers, tries to throw off its assailant. Eyes wide in terror, the deer bleats. Wolf sinks its fangs into the deer's side, rips and tears at the deer's skin and flesh.

It is brutal to human eyes. The one seeing the kill scorns the wolf for putting an end to the deer, a creature of grace, beauty and gentility. The witness grieves for the stricken deer.

Wolf and his kin showed the first man and woman how to watch and listen. Whatever they wanted to see or hear was there in front of them, taking place every day, every year.

Our ancestors saw and watched Loons, and in them devotion and fidelity to each other. Inseparable they are, the way that mates ought to be. Even within sight and hearing, separated only by a short flight, they call out to each other "Don't leave me." Should one wander and not return to the side of its mate, the other will go in search, inconsolable, afraid to face the coming days alone.

Loons care for one another, but as nestlings they've been known to kill each other to gain sole attention and place next to their parents. Jealous they are in their infancy. Only later do they learn caring.

Loons and other birds and creatures elicit, or ought to elicit our admiration for their industry and foresight; crows earn our low opinion. They don't work. They raid the nests of smaller birds whenever they can, and get their food by eating their eggs. Lacking courage, they wait till the parents are gone from the nest before setting on the unguarded nest. Should the nesting pair return to their nest before the crow has destroyed their eggs, or before it has reached the nest, the pair, though smaller, can and will drive off the larger. It is David and Goliath enacted over and over in every part of the land. Yet the crow persists; it cannot learn. Robins, kingbirds and other smaller birds know this. But it still takes courage on the part of the smaller to meet far larger than they are.

By lakeshores are birds of immense beauty and grace, but inside their souls and spirits burns and smolders selfishness. In the beginning they were given a gift, just as every other being was given a gift. Every insect, bird, animal, fish shared the gift that they had received from Kitchi-Manitou, all except for the seagull. For its refusal to share willingly its gift with others, the seagull has been condemned to eat decay and to keep the waters clear. To this day seagulls will fight their kin and kind for scraps of rotting offal, and swallow it whole lest another seagull snatch it from them.

Turn yet to another scene in another time ... spring. It is the courting season; the sun courts the earth; grouse, orioles strut, flaunt their feathers, drum, dance and sing to attract a mate who acts coy. Such vanity! Such coyness!

On the ground at your feet are ants. All day they work, going to and fro like a moving necklace of beads into the earth and out again. Only at night do they rest and maybe even play; no one knows. In a pond beavers fell trees, build dams and their lodges and store food for the coming winter. Diligent they are, minding their own business. They know that they must provide for their winter needs. There will be ample time for rest come winter. Beavers can teach anyone who wants to learn much about the habit of work and foresight.

There is a certain order in the heavens and on earth. Nights follow days; spring follows winter, and is itself followed by summer and the autumn. In the spring all things are born anew; they grow, decline and then are no more.

Geese, finches, orioles and butterflies live by the cycle of the seasons. They go south when days grow short and cold, return when arctic temperatures give way to longer days and warmer. On their return to their summering homes, they mate, give birth to young, bring their offspring to maturity, and then once more go to the warmer south.

Our ancestors watched the insects, birds, animals.

Just before they begin their southern journey, geese gather in great flocks. Each flock gathered behind one leader. Though there were many leaders, there were no contests between them as to leadership or number of followers. Geese were free to follow the leader of their own choosing. So do geese live in harmony with the seasons and each other.

The way humans should live.

Geese, caribou, cougars, and butterflies come and go, wherever they please, whenever they choose. They do not ask permission of anyone. And being free, they are equal. Cardinals, tanagers, sparrows give thanks to Kitchi-Manitou and Mother Earth the day through during the season in thanksgiving for the bounty at hand. Birds and animals have a sense of ownership of the land that they occupy during their lives.

What our ancestors learned of the land, the wind, the fire and the waters, the beetles, the hawks, the wolverines and the otters is revelation, no less than is dream. Through the high places and low, Kitchi-Manitou shows us, speaks to us. Our ancestors watched and listened. The land was their book. The land has given us our understandings, beliefs, perceptions, laws, customs. It has bent and shaped our notions of human nature, conduct and the Great Laws. And our ancestors tried to abide by those laws. The land has given us everything. It is more than a book.

PREFACE

The land meant much to the Six Nations peoples and to the other North American Indians. The affection and respect they had came from their bond with the earth. Their existence depended upon the earth. From their perspective their kinship with the land, sea, air and fire was one of utter dependence, as a child clings to its mother.

When negotiators offered money for land, Crowfoot, a Cree, rejected the money, saying:

> Our land is more valuable than your money. It will last forever. It will not even perish by the flames of fire. As long as the sun shines and the waters flow, this land will be here to give life to men and animals; therefore, we cannot sell this land. It was put here for us by the Great Spirit and we cannot sell it because it does not belong to us. You can count your money and burn it within the nod of a buffalo's head, but only the Great Spirit can count the grains of sand and the blades of grass of these plains. As a present to you, we will give you anything we have that you can take with you, but the land, never.

Smohalla, a Nez Perce, expressed his regard for the earth by saying:

> You ask me to plow the ground. Shall I take a knife and tear my mother's breast? Then when I die she will not take me to her bosom to rest.

> You ask me to dig for stone. Shall I dig under her skin for her bones? Then when I die I cannot enter her body to be born again.

> You ask me to cut grass and make hay and sell it and be rich like white men. But how dare I cut off my mother's hair?

For what is the earth that we live on? By itself it is nothing more than rock, water, air and fire, barren, uninhabitable. But with trees and shrubs, plants and flowers, insects, birds, animals and fish, the earth comes alive. The rock carved into mountains, hills, valleys, scarps and meadows; the water, falling as rain from above, flowing as rivers, cascading over falls, forming pools and lakes, radiate beauty. The air moving or rushing over trees or lakes resonates music. And the fire as sun or lightning lends light and warmth. These elements, fused as one to form the earth, bring good and beauty into being, growth and life. The land is everything.

The land sustains life and has within it meanings. It is for men and women to discover what the meanings are and to profit by them. The earth has what men and women need to grow in body and in spirit.

Tatanga Mani, a Stoney, held the same sentiments as did Red Jacket with respect to the land. He wrote:

> Oh yes. I went to the White Man's schools. I learned to read from school books, newspapers, and the Bible. But in time I found that these were not enough. Civilized people depend too much on man-made printed pages. I turn to the Great Spirit's book which is the whole of creation. You can read a big part of that book if you study nature. You know, if you take all your books, lay them out under the sun, and let the snow and rain and insects work on them for a while, there will be nothing left. But the Great Spirit has provided you and me with an opportunity for study in nature's university: the forests, the rivers, the mountains, and the animals, which include us.

What men and women discover about the earth, life, and themselves is revelation no less than those received by the men named in the bible. Men and women watching the plants, insects, birds and animals will or ought to learn something. When they do, their eyes, ears, mind and heart are opened at once to something that they didn't know before. This is revelation. It is as if it were the Earth telling them something that they didn't before know.

To the North American Indians, studying the earth and listening to it was the way they learned. This way of learning is in many respects better than learning from a book that stimulates only the eye and the mind, whereas the earth stimulates not only sight, but smell, hearing, taste, touch, and intuition.

It was by watching, listening and sensing the earth that the North American Indians came to believe in a Creator. Tatanka-ohitika, a Dakota, said:

> When I was 10 years of age I looked at the land and the rivers, the sky above, and the animals around me and could not fail to realize that they were made by some great power. I was so anxious to understand this power that I questioned the trees and the bushes. It seemed as though the flowers were staring at me, and I wanted to ask them, 'Who made you?' I looked at the moss-covered stones; some of them seemed to have the features of a man, but they could not answer me. Then I had a dream, and in my dream one of these small stones appeared to me and told me that the maker of all was Wakan tanka and that in order to honour him I must honour his works in nature.

For manifesting the existence of a Creator and revealing answers about the Great Laws, right and wrong, and the soul and spirit world, the earth is sacred. It is holy in its entirety.

Wakan Tanka, The Great Mystery, is kind and generous. The land that the Creator made was intended for everyone residing in the territory set aside for each nation and for each species. The land was meant for insects, birds, animals, fish and humans, and for generations to come. Within the territory set aside for nations, individuals and families occupied land that they regarded as their home "ae-indauyaun", and which their neighbours granted as belonging to them, "ae-indauwaut."

"The Great Spirit is our father, but the earth is our mother" Big

Thunder, a Wabanaki, said.

> She nourishes us; that which we put into the ground she returns to
> us, and healing plants she gives us likewise. If we are wounded, we
> go to our mother and seek to lay the wounded part against her to be
> healed. Animals too, do this; they lay their wounds to the earth.
> When we go hunting, it is not our arrow that kills the moose, how-
> ever powerful the bow, it is nature that kills him. The arrow sticks in
> his hide and, like all living things, the moose goes to our mother to
> be healed. He seeks to lay his wound against the earth, and thus he
> drives the arrow further in. Meanwhile, I follow. He is out of sight
> but I put my ear to a tree in the forest, and that brings me the sound,
> and I hear the moose make his next leap, and I follow. The moose
> stops again for the pain of the arrow and he rubs his side upon the
> earth and drives the arrow farther in....

When we are sick we go to our Mother Earth for medicine and comfort.
When we die we return into her bosom. Mother Earth takes us back into
her body and soul.

The question that Tatanka-ohitika asked "Who made the earth?" was
asked by countless other boys and girls, men and women. "How?" they
next asked.

CREATION

Some scientists tell us the gasses present in space reacted and "BOOM!"
exploded, showering the heavens with stars, comets, planets, suns, moons,
dust and vapours. This is known as the "Big Bang" theory. But not all
scientists, astronomers, or physicists accept this theory. There are a number
of prominent scientists who suppose that there is someone, something that
created the gasses that exploded. And that someone, something is The
Creator, The First Cause.

While the North American Indians treasured their bond with Mother

Earth, West Europeans, on the other hand, had long ago cut the umbilical cord that attached them to the land. The monarch they were told, and so they believed, owned the land and everything upon it. God had given it directly to the monarch. He only could have title to the land. No ordinary person could ever own land. Though they could till the land for a lord, vassals of a king, peasants, serfs and slaves could not keep their harvest for their own use. The lord, and after him the clergyman, took a portion of the harvest and left the tiller of soil with a smaller share of the crop than would meet his family's needs in the coming winter. The men and the women who tilled the soils were not free nor independent, but were no more than mere chattels, subject to and owned by the king. As mere labourers, men and women had no stake in the land. They could never understand it and so could not love it. They could only resent it. Those who could escape tilling the soil fled to cities to start life anew in a setting far from the land.

The churches themselves did their share in fostering a low regard for the earth. In burial rites, the clergyman pronounced to the departed "Dust thou art and unto Dust shalt thou return." If they were to say "A son (daughter) of The Great Spirit thou art, and unto The Great Spirit art thou returning" or some similar expression it would not be   anathema, and it would be no offence to our Maker.

To the church and society then, land was dust and the hinterland a wilderness inhabited by wild beasts. God could not dwell in the wilderness. No mountain or valley, no matter how beautiful, was fit for God. So the people captured God, imprisoned Him in Tabernacles and Arks, and kept Him imprisoned in churches, synagogues, mosques and temples, guarded by clergymen who allowed Him a weekly visit. Land could never be made holy by the presence of God or angels or saints.

Except for farmers and hunters and fishermen who make their living off the land and waterways, this generation has little to do with land. Men and women drive to the supermarket for tinned and packaged meats and vegetables; they watch videos and television, listen to radios and tapes; they read books for information and recreation; ill, they speed to a doctor, pick up their medication at a drug store and return home. While in town for whatever purpose, men and women shepherd their children into some fast food outlet for a treat consisting of prefabricated, greasy ground meat sandwiched between two pieces of a flavourless bun. That is the outing, the picnic. On the way home, children play video games. At home there are computers to play. City dwellers live in high rises or in homes built and situated in developments given exotic names: Wiltshire Estates, Bayview Forest. But these developments are nothing more than man-made concrete canyons. Concrete is the reality that has replaced land.

At school, children learn little about the land, the earth. If they study geography, they may learn that the heavenly bodies, planets, suns, moons, stars and life began with an explosion. Their texts refer to the earth and the land, its features as habitat, environment, landscape, wasteland, eco-system, real estate, resources, land mass, jungle. City people look on the land and the country as park, wild, resorts, playgrounds; soil, dirt, dust, mud. Rains, thunderstorms, blizzards, tornadoes, forest fires are bad because they spoil week-ends and damage property that cost huge amounts of money.

Words used in referring to land reflect attitudes and views of those who have little to do with land. These words and expressions represent a low regard for the land and other forms of life.

Even if the modern generation is not as close to the earth as its ances-tors used to be, it ought to study the earth and the land anew and from a fresh perspective, not just for the sake of study or to satisfy curriculum guidelines, but to understand our source of life and well-being.

Perhaps this generation and its governments will take the pollution of the air, the waters and the soils more seriously. Smog hangs over cities, poisons are dumped in lakes and rivers, chemical fertilizers and pesticides are spread on the ground to enhance growth, but kill insects and birds and are absorbed in fruit, vegetables and grasses.

Today few people, excepting those who live in the far north, read the stars, comets, sun, moon, aurora borealis, or listen to the owls, nighthawks, wolves, thunder, or study the water currents, the colour, the formation and the height of clouds, or take note of the time of arrival of summer birds, when they cease their callings, how low to the ground bees nest, how busy the squirrels, how soon the geese flew south, how long the trilliums flowered, how tall the grasses grew. To know what the weather is going to be the next day, they listen to the radio and believe every word that the meteorologist utters.

In the past, men and women looked to the clergy for an understanding of "the book" and its meanings; today they look to scientists, experts and researchers, who conduct their studies in a university or museum laboratory, and who report their findings, limited to fact and data, in scientific journals.

North American Indians were as keen observers as the scientists of today. But, unlike modern scientists who conduct their research indoors, North American Indians conducted their studies in the natural setting of the earth under natural conditions. Nor did they limit their reports to fact and data. They went beyond that. They used fact and data as bases for stories that exemplified something of human nature and conduct to be imitated or spurned. It was through stories drawn from the dramas taking place on the earth among other living creatures that tribal teachers passed along the tribe's values, beliefs, teachings, traditions, understandings... everything. Manitous, insects, birds, animals, fish and humans were characters in these stories, just as they play large roles in life.

North American Indians didn't have books such as European and other races had, but they had the greatest book of all, "Mother Earth," a book that preceded all other books.

I have set the chapters in this text in the order in which the Anishinaubae people believed that creation was carried out, by stages. And I've written down as many stories in each chapter as would, I hope, exemplify what Red Jacket meant when he said, "...to us He has given the earth."

MOTHER EARTH - MIZZU-KUMMICK-QUAE

CREATION

According to Anishinaubae mythology, Kitchi-Manitou had a wondrous vision. In that instant a rattle began to sound in the everlasting darkness. At first the sound was faint and weak, for it was made by the tiniest seed of sound. Then it grew and exploded in a thunderous blast that shattered the everlasting stillness and darkness. The seed of sound was the seed of life. It burst its casement and shot forth rock, fire, water and wind that became the sun, the moon, the stars, the planets and the earth that hung suspended in the skies. Then Kitchi-Manitou created Manitous and assigned them certain duties. After them, Kitchi-Manitou made plants of every kind, insects, birds, animals, fish and last, humans. To each The Creator assigned a place, a time, and a service to perform.

THE FLOOD

There were four Keepers of the winds, weather, and the seasons who dwelt, as their names suggest, at each of the four cardinal points: Akeewaedin (North), Waubun (East), Zhauwun (South), and Ae-pungishi-mook or Ningobee-anung (West). As Keepers they often passed over the land to see what they needed to do to carry out their duties to the earth.

It was on one of these tours that Ae-pungishimook saw and chose Winonah to be his wife. They had four sons: Maudjee-kawiss, Pukawiss, Cheeby-aub-oozoo, and Nana'b'oozoo (also known as Nanabush). Each son had a duty to perform for his people. Maudjee-kawiss was a hunter, a man of action who performed deeds that made history and were worth remembering. Pukawiss was an actor, entertainer who performed dances that dramatized what happened in life. He made festivals and wore fine, bright clothing. Cheeby-aub-oozoo was a musician. When he chanted, he did so with the beat of a drum. He could make the birds listen with his flute as he imitated them and the winds and the rain. Cheeby-aub-oozoo could talk to the manitous in dream.

Nana'b'oozoo, the last born, was a manitou like his brothers. Yet for most of his life he acted more like the most ordinary of human beings; impulsive, timid, lazy, proud, greedy, dishonest, curious, disrespectful, envious, boastful, lascivious. More often than not he gave in to his human feelings. When Nana'b'oozoo's failings got the better of him, he exemplified the tremendous forces that humans face within themselves, and must overcome in order to carry out their intentions. Like most human beings, he meant well. On those occasions when Nana'b'oozoo overcame his failings and the forces against him and succeeded in attaining his intent, his achievement was an extraordinary one akin to a miracle.

But for the most part, Nana'b'oozoo bumbled and blundered along the Path of Life, achieving his triumphs more often by chance and bluster.

Like every man and woman, Nana'b'oozoo had a great deal to learn and so many obstacles to overcome.

Wolf watched Nana'b'oozoo bumbling around for a while in the forest. She felt sorry for this half-manitou, half-man. He had so much to learn about himself and the forest. So she took it upon herself to act as this man's mentor and his companion.

She soon annoyed and embarrassed Nana'b'oozoo with her questions that showed how little he knew. He gave all the wrong answers and showed how much he had to learn and how much more the wolf knew. Nana'b'oozoo didn't like being shown up, made to look stupid, especially in front of the wolf cubs.

As they went along, Nana'b'oozoo made up his mind to get back at the wolf, bring her down a few notches from her perch. He'd play a trick on her for making him look foolish.

In the early days of spring, just as the river ice was breaking up, Nana'b'oozoo got his chance to have his revenge without hurting his mentor. They were standing on the bank of a large river trying to figure out how to get to the other side safely and in the shortest time possible. In the wolf's opinion, they would either have to walk up-stream or down to get to the nearest fording place. Nana'b'oozoo argued that it wasn't necessary to travel so far to cross over to the far bank.

They would cross over to the other bank by using poles as bridges to go from one flow of ice to another. "Lay the pole down from ice flow to ice flow, run across on the pole. Take the pole with you until you're on the other side. That's the way human beings do it," Nana'b'oozoo explained. "It'll save a lot of time and effort."

Nana'b'oozoo even helped the wolf fetch a pole and lay it down from the bank to the nearest cake of ice that was floating by. "Be careful" he warned his companion. "I'll be right behind with my own pole."

Right from the first the wolf had difficulty balancing on the round pole that was rolling and moving. On shore Nana'b'oozoo chortled as he watched the wolf fling her legs and tail wildly about as if she were walking on hot coals or a tight rope. In a few moments the wolf toppled off the log with a yelp and slipped into the river.

Now was Nana'b'oozoo's chance to do something for his friend. Nana'b'oozoo went from ice flow to ice flow using his pole as a bridge.

He looked down into the river. He saw nothing; he called but no one answered. While he was standing on the ice it cracked under his weight. He sank into the ice cold waters. Nana'b'oozoo managed to make it ashore. As he lay on the bank, his bones and teeth rattling, Nana'b'oozoo suspected that the wolf dove out of sight to double-cross him into disaster.

When he'd recovered his breath and his strength, Nana'b'oozoo, hurt and furious, walked back and forth along the river bank looking for the wolf, meaning to skin the wolf alive and tan her hide. While Nana'b'oozoo was pacing to and fro, calling for the wolf, a raven came along and told him that the Great Lynx had pulled the wolf underwater and carried her off to her den.

Nana'b'oozoo wept for days. Eventually, Nana'b'oozoo's grief subsided. He went home, not to stay, but to tell his grandmother and his neighbours that he was going to kill the Great Lynx and that he'd return home only with the Great Lynx's skin.

Not knowing where the Great Lynx dwelt, Nana'b'oozoo asked everyone he saw for directions. He got little help except to learn that his enemy dwelt underwater, an odd place for a land being. Before long everyone knew that Nana'b'oozoo was hunting for the Great Lynx.

After paddling all day on the first day of his pursuit, Nana'b'oozoo went ashore on the bank of the river that wound around and through the valleys of a mountainous land. Following his evening meal, Nana'b'oozoo settled down to sleep under his canoe to keep the rain that was beginning to fall from drenching him.

Nana'b'oozoo woke up with a start. He was lying in water. The rain was drumming on his canoe. The river had risen and was overflowing its banks. He moved his makeshift shelter up the mountainside. The rain was coming down harder. No sooner, so it seemed, had he gone to sleep than the water was once more at his shoulders. Again and again Nana'b'oozoo had to move. Each time that he moved his shelter, Nana'b'oozoo damned the owls for not giving warning of coming rain as they were supposed to have done. Angry and near panic, Nana'b'oozoo momentarily forgot his

canoe in his latest decampment. During this lapse in his attention, his
canoe floated away out of reach.

In the twilight at dawn, Nana'b'oozoo found that he was on top of a
mountain. It was still raining, the water still rising. Soon the pinnacle on
which he was perched would be covered and he would be finished.

A log floated nearby. Nana'b'oozoo swam for it, put his arms around
it and hung on and uttered a prayer in thanksgiving. He was saved, at
least for the time being. He looked around. All about him were logs,
stumps, branches, grasses, each one occupied by one or more survivors.

"Nana'b'oozoo! How long is it going to rain? What are we going to
do?" they called out.

Yes! What were they going to do? Nana'b'oozoo didn't know.

He was going to die. He was going to drown. He cried. He prayed.

The animals and the birds on board their logs and branches pushed
them together to form a raft for Nana'b'oozoo.

The muskrat brought up some soil from the bottom of the sea. He
gave the ball of mud to Nana'b'oozoo who didn't know what to do with it.

"Breathe upon it," the animals urged Nana'b'oozoo. Even though he
couldn't see the point in breathing upon the ball of mud, Nana'b'oozoo
did what the animals asked him to do. To his astonishment, the ball grew.

RE-CREATION - ANISHINAUBAE-AKI

With a single breath of life the ball of mud became an island and then
a continent.

To learn how large their land was, Nana'b'oozoo sent a pigeon aloft.
After but a short flight the pigeon returned. He told Nana'b'oozoo that
he could see the ends of the island but that it was growing. In
Nana'b'oozoo's opinion the world wasn't yet large enough. Next he sent
the raven, who ascended to an even higher altitude than had the pigeon.
On coming down, raven reported that he'd never seen a larger island and
that it was pushing in every direction. Nana'b'oozoo shook his head. The
land wasn't large enough for them all. Sometime later he sent the eagle
off. The eagle soared up into the sky to get an eagle-eye's view of the

land below. When the eagle alighted, he said that he could not see the ends of the earth though he had ascended to a height higher than a mountain.

If the eagle could not see the extent of the earth from the clouds, the earth must be large enough to allow the survivors to return to their homes and to resume their lives that had been disrupted by the flood. "You may now go home. The flood's over. You'll be safe," Nana' b'oozoo told them.

Sometime after the flood waters subsided, Nana'b'oozoo set out to see for himself how large was the land that Kitchi-Manitou had given the Anishinaubae peoples. What did it look like? As his guide and companion, Nana'b'oozoo invited a wolf, who went along willingly, anxious to see the world. Not knowing that Nana'b'oozoo had nearly killed his sister, Wolf still trusted the man.

Where did Nana'b'oozoo and Wolf set out on their tour? It could have been anywhere. He left stories of his travels with the Anishinaubae-peoples that he visited. Many old people still remember his name, and smile whenever they recall Nana'b'oozoo.

The Anishinaubae-people in Northwestern Quebec remember him, although that part of Anishinaubae-aki wasn't then called Quebec which means "closed off" in both the Anishinaubae and Mushkeego languages. The name came later. That name was derived from a reference to a point in the St. Lawrence River that appears to be blocked off or closed.

Nana'b'oozoo and his companion Wolf went down the Gatineau Valley, hunting on both sides of the river as far as the Ottawa River. They followed the Ottawa River downstream but turned back at the border of Six Nations country. From the confluence of the Ottawa and Gatineau Rivers, Nana'b'oozoo and Wolf cut across the Kawartha Highlands (Gauwautae) to Chemong and Curve Lake, then on to Lake Scugog and on to Lake Simcoe and Couchiching. They continued in a westerly direction along the southern shores of Georgian Bay, then called Waussaugummauh, The Shining Sea. At Numae-Weequaedoong, now Owen Sound, they trekked across in a southwest direction to the shores of another Great Sea, Lake Huron, Odauwau-gummauh, then southward to Wauwi-autinoong, Lake St. Clair.

Nana'b'oozoo and his companion could have gone further south, but the land belonged to, and was already occupied by, other people. Besides, it was getting too warm. From the Detroit area they went on to Chicago, Milwaukee, Green Bay, southwest again, then on up to Duluth, then on to Bimidji. They went no further. Beyond that the land was flat, treeless, lakeless. Skirting the land of the Great Plains that made them feel exposed, Nana'b'oozoo and Wolf went as far north as Lake Winnipeg. Here they wheeled about and followed a course northeast that skirted muskeg country, the land of the Cree, until they returned to their starting point in Northwestern Quebec.

From start to finish it had taken Nana'b'oozoo and Wolf several years to make the circuit around this vast tract of land. What prolonged Nana'b'oozoo's odyssey were numerous side excursions and extended visits with Anishinaubae villages, towns and large settlements. Adding to the distance around the homeland of the Anishinaubae was the course of the border. At no stretch was the border straight or fixed. It wound and meandered like a river. When Nana'b'oozoo didn't return home after his first year of absence, his kin and neighbours assumed that he was dead. His return was unexpected but welcome.

The land was rugged, beautiful to behold Nana'b'oozoo said.

There were mountains, not so lofty as to be snow covered as are the Rocky Mountains out west or the Appalachians and the Adirondacks to the east, but imposing in their own right, deserving the name of mountains. These were the depositories of gold, silver, copper, iron, nickel, and the realm of eagles, the nesting places of thunderbirds, the dwelling places of manitous and the watersheds of springs and rivers. Bordering the Prairies are the Great Turtle Mountains in North Dakota. In Northern Minnesota are the Itasca Highlands that serve as the watershed for the mighty Mississippi River. The Porcupine Mountain range in North Eastern Wisconsin and North Western Michigan is a storehouse of iron ore and other metals and ores. Along the northern shores of Lake Superior and on across Northern Ontario and spreading into Quebec is one continuous mass of highland wherein are stored gold, silver, nickel, copper, fool's gold. On the sheer walls of the Agawa Canyon in the Highlands Agawa, Anishinaubae holy men and women inscribed the messages they received from the manitous through dream. These places were holy. And on out-crops in such distant places as in Quetico, and near Curve Lake and north of Peterborough are Teaching Rocks inscribed with glyphs. There are other Teaching Rocks, known only to a few old people.

Over thousands of years, rains, melting snow and waters from small and large lakes, surging over the earth and coursing to lower levels swept gravel and carved valleys, gorges, falls and canyons, swamps, pools and ponds, the dwelling and feeding places for birds and animals and small creatures. In summer the valleys are lush with plants, grasses filled with medicines. Come autumn, mists rise and soften shapes and colours. The Gatineau, Mississippi, Nipissing, Madawaska, Bad River Valleys and thou-sands of others are Mother Earth's lifelines.

From Niagara Falls to the western tip of Manitoulin Island, the dwelling place of manitous, the west side of the land is higher than the other as if the eastern side had dropped under some great weight.

Parts of Michigan, Wisconsin and Southern Ontario are grasslands, flat and lush with hay, straw, goldenrod, like the prairies.

Within this vast Anishinaubae territory are six great bodies of water; pure, clear, fresh. Our ancestors ranked Georgian Bay as one of the great lakes. Lesser in size but not in importance to the people who lived on or near its shores were lakes Timagami, Simcoe, Nipissing, Rainy, Nipigon, Red, Net, Winnipeg, Flambeau, Mille Lacs, and Eel. Still smaller were thousands of other lakes and ponds that were formed by the fall of a gigantic thunderbird ball that burst upon landing. It exploded, sending showers of rocks into the sky which fell upon the earth, leaving craters large and small that filled up with water.

Rivers that drained the watersheds were arteries that delivered the water which cleansed and nourished Mother Earth. One of the continent's mightiest rivers is the Mississippi which originates in Northern Minnesota and flows south into the Gulf of Mexico. The St. Mary's River, a relatively short river, drains Lake Superior into Lake Huron and Georgian Bay. The St. Clair channels the waters of Lake Huron into Lake St. Clair and on into Lake Erie. The waters of Erie are then carried by the Niagara River over Niagara Falls, through a gorge, into Lake Ontario. The waters of these great inland seas are last carried off, churning and roaring, down the St. Lawrence into the Atlantic Ocean.

In the lakes and rivers are countless islands, great and small. Manitoulin Island was well known as the Dwelling Place of the Manitous. Michillmackinac Island, The Great Turtle was named to commemorate the service that The Great Turtle performed in the creation and re-creation of the earth. The Sleeping Giant just offshore at the Lakehead is really Nana'b'oozoo, who was turned into a rock in sadness when his people turned their backs on him. There is an island in the middle of Lake Mindemoya on Manitoulin Island. Nana'b'oozoo left his grandmother there to die. Several days after abandoning her, he had a change of heart, returned and took her with him. After a band of Anishinaubaek returned from a trek to the east, they settled on a group of islands, now called the Apostle Islands, just off the shores of Red Cliff reservation.

NEIGHBOURS

In occupying a large territory the Anishinaubae peoples had many neighbours living next door as it were. Most of their neighbours, Cree, Naskapi, Shawnee, Kickapoo, Menominee, Illiniwuk, spoke a similar language and shared a common outlook. They were kin who seldom quarrelled. With their other neighbours, The Six Nations, Winnebago, and Dakota, the relationship was touchy. Trespass into the other's territory sparked skirmishes; macho young men anxious to flaunt their daring provoked altercations and retaliations. The relationship was akin to fighting cocks.

The Cree may have been closest in language and in tradition to the Anishinaubae. They occupied land north of the Anishinaubae territory, extending as far east as did the Anishinaubae territory and much farther west, as far west as the Peace River in northern Alberta. Theirs was the land of the jackpine and scrub, caribou and moose, long in winter and short in summer. The Anishinaubaek felt sorry for their kin for their grant of land, in jest calling them "swamp dwellers." The Cree were neither envious of the Anishinaubae for their land nor slighted by the name given them. They grinned and retorted "you sound funny when you talk (chipp-awae), and you're not tough enough to survive in the north."

At the most northeastern limit of the Anishinaubaeaki were the Naskapi. Their land was more like that of the Cree, and their spirit and character were as rugged as their land and their way of life.

To the east, along the St. Lawrence and on the north-west shores of Lake Erie and Lake Ontario, but chiefly on the southeastern lands in what is now New York State were the "Naudawaek." They called themselves "Houdenissaunee," the people. Primarily they raised crops of corn, beans and squash for their livelihood. Even small skirmishes disrupted and threatened the supply of food they obtained by tilling. The Houdenissaunee foresaw that the only way to reduce these fights was by forming a federation or a league of nations. First they established the five nations, a union among themselves. Next they admitted the Tuscarora to constitute the Six Nations. Their aim was to invite the Anishinaubae nation, as well as others to form one great federation to bring about peace.

To the south in Ohio, Illinois, and Indiana were the Shauwunee, Kickapoo, Sauk and Fox people, kindred in language, belief, custom and institution. Their dreams were modest. They yearned to live and provide for their families, to live in peace with their neighbours and in friendship with the manitous. Tecumseh, perceiving the danger to the Indian owner-ship of the land posed by the non-stop influx of West Europeans into the interior, went from nation to nation inviting them to unite in one grand alliance to stop the white people from taking even more Indian territory. He didn't succeed, but he and others played a much greater role in preventing the Americans from taking Canada in 1812 than he and his warriors have been given credit. Another hunter, a family man who was vilified for resisting the American cavalry in order to keep his land and to protect his people was Black Hawk, a Sauk and Fox. He and his people did not wish to surrender their land.

At the headwaters of the Mississippi lived the Dakota. The land that Wakan Tanka, their name for the Great Mystery, allotted to them was prairie, flat, open, almost treeless, a yellow sea of coarse grass and flowers. The bison was their staff of life, millions of them. With the countless bison, the Dakota peoples would never starve. Unlike the Anishinaubaek, the Dakotas could never live in any but open areas where they could be free in spirit. And because the Dakota had a unique and close kinship with the bison and the earth, they practiced a spectacular ritual to the bison and the sun in a ceremony called the Sun Dance. The ritual originated a long time ago and is as old as the Dakota Nation itself. So numerous were the bison that the Dakota took them for granted, creatures to be slaughtered simply to serve human needs. Killing one, 10, 100 made no difference. Wakan Tanka was offended, and recalled the bison into hiding. Without the bison, the Dakota were like castaways whose days were numbered. They prayed for salvation and they won Wakan Tanka's compassion. For returning the buffalo to their lives, the Dakota were to perform the Sun Dance as a reminder of their kinship and debt to the bison and Father Sun. They were men and women of peace, but would retaliate when provoked, as quick and as fierce as a badger to drive off an intruder.

In the long ago our ancestors and their neighbours were more part of the earth than they are now, much more familiar with the rivers, birds, animals, weather, and stars.

They slept on cedar boughs spread on the ground.

They walked wherever they went, or travelled by canoe just off shore on lakes and rivers.

They studied the earth and knew where deer and other animals bedded down, where and what they ate, where they gave birth, summered, wintered, and their range and enemies.

They heard and listened to owls, hawks, loons, wolves and foxes and understood what they said.

They smelled pine, spruce, blossoms, sweet grass and tobacco.

They tasted and ate corn, wild rice, maple syrup, pumpkins, squashes and honey.

They watched buds become leaves, blossoms become fruit, tadpoles become frogs, and a chrysalis become caterpillar, cocoon, and then butterfly.

They felt the prick of thistles, the sting of bees, the softness of down, the warmth of fire and the bite of frost.

They sensed danger, the need of others in distant places, the presence of spirits, and the medicine people could summon and communicate with the manitous.

They set their courses at night by the stars.

They were keen observers, taking note especially of relationships between birds, animals, plants and insects, and habitat; between the aspect of the sun, moon, the formation and colour of the clouds and the direction of the wind and the weather; between rain, light, heat and growth.

They studied the character of their quarry, how they got on with each other, how they cared for their offspring, how geese came together and followed a leader, how they eluded pursuit. Dumb, animals were not.

Some were models of virtue, in the care of their offspring in the exercise of leadership, in their steadfastness to their mate, in organization, in abiding by the Great Laws of Nature. Others practiced the worst of human traits, selfishness, sloth, anger, deceit. Animals were not to be underestimated; in some respects they outdid some humans in caring for their young and living in harmony with their neighbours and the earth. In still other respects, strength, speed, sight, hearing, smell, the animals were better endowed. To bring down a deer, a moose, a goose, an otter, took all the hunter's cunning, patience and strength.

The land was a land of plenty; birds, animals, fish, fruit, corn and wild rice beyond reckoning. As plentiful as was food and game, men and women still had to take risks and to shed sweat in pursuit of deer, moose, and to harvest corn, squash and wild rice. They had to master their short-comings, to take on the rugged land with its distances, and endure the heat waves, the violent storms, and the snows deep, the winters cold and long.

To meet the challenge made them men and women. The land provided everything that they needed to live; it gave them perceptions and understandings of the spirit, things unseen.

THE PIPE OF PEACE

There was so much to be thankful for; for individual men and women and children, for families and for the community. For children there were parents, grandparents, everyone; for adults there was the sun, the earth, the winds.

In private, men and women gave thanks to Kitchi-Manitou for favours by offering tobacco and expressing their thoughts and feelings in their own way. There was no formality; anyone could do it, anytime a person received a benefit. "Thank you! I have nothing to give you in return except my gratitude and tobacco."

As a community the people had derived, in addition to the necessities for life, freedom, land, character, and their understandings and perceptions. The land gave them their identity and heritage. The land had given them more than they could say. At best and at most, they could only say, "We give thanks."

And to express the depth of their obligation, they blended their thanksgiving with their petitions in the Pipe of Peace ceremony.

The first whiff of smoke was offered skyward to The Master of Life and Creator of all beings:

"Let us as one in thought and in heart
Offer our thanksgiving to The Great Mystery
For life and all good things."
The second whiff was down to Mother Earth:
"We offer thanksgiving as well
To the earth, Mother of us all

For having given us food and drink,
        shelter and freedom
        medicines and colours
        music and beauty
        kin and neighbours
        teachings and laws."

To the north:
    "We offer the tobacco of thanksgiving
    To those that abide in the north
    Guardians of our stories and understandings."

To the east:
    "We offer the tobacco of thanksgiving
    To those that abide in the east,
    Guardians of youth and progenitors of youth and hope."

To the south:
    "We offer thanksgiving
    To those that dwell in the south
    Custodians of life, growth and plenty."

To the west:
    "We offer thanksgiving
    To those that abide in the west
    Grandfathers, grandmothers
    For marking well the Path of Life."

WEATHER

Ages ago there was only one season in Anishinaubae-Aki, summer. It was always fair and warm, with just the right amount of rain. Our ancestors didn't have to make or wear warm clothing, huddle in heated dwellings or collect wood and stand by a fireside. In this land stood a single tree that was bent with the weight of every fruit, vegetable, seed and nut imaginable. With food within reach, no one ever went hungry. The word hunger did not exist. Anishinaubae-Aki was Paradise.

Life was easy, the way people would like life to be. There was no such experience as hardship.

Kitchi-Manitou had made life too easy. People didn't care for the land; they took the Tree of Life for granted. Eat. Drink. Dance. Sleep. That was life. By planting the Tree of Life and Plenty, Kitchi-Manitou had done too much for men and women, so much that men and women had little to do for themselves. No one, not even Kitchi-Manitou, could know what men and women were capable of.

Kitchi-Manitou called the chiefs and the people together and directed them to "cut down the Tree of Life. And cut the limbs and branches and shoots, and plant these in the earth."

"Why?" the people asked, giving their Tree of Life a little serious thought for the first time. "How will we eat?"

"The shoots and the branches that you plant will grow and bear whatever you may want to eat. And the trees and plants that grow will yield only one harvest each year. From now on you will have to sweat and shiver, chafe your hands, suffer setback and heartbreak to earn your meal. Only by work will you learn what you are capable of and what the tree is worth."

The Anishinaubae people cut down the Tree of Life and planted its limbs, branches and shoots that grew into plants and trees, shrubs and grasses, which yielded fruit and vegetables, seeds and nuts and saps of every kind.

SUMMER AND WINTER

Up to this time there was only one season, summer; and two kinds of weather, sunny and rainy, with rain falling every few days and in just the right quantities, enough to keep trees and plants green and lush.

Now, there dwelt in the north Abi-boon, the Winter Spirit, who never ventured outside his snow-bound territory, quietly minding his own business and leaving others to mind theirs.

After so many years confined to the north, Winter Spirit may have suffered snow fever. Whatever the reason, Winter Spirit wandered further south than was usual for him. It was the first time that he had done so, and the first time that he'd seen humans, birds, animals, forests, lakes. He gawked, finding it hard to take in what he saw, and quite unable to rein in his curiosity, which got away from him.

"Ahneen! Boozhoo!" he shouted to grab the attention of the

strange creatures in front of his eyes.

Winter Spirit's voice was no ordinary voice. But he didn't know this. It whined and chilled everything within its reach and range. Hearing and feeling its cold force, birds started, squawked and flew off; some animals went underground; human beings caught off guard scrambled to cover themselves from the chilling draft. They built warm shelters and made fires within. Leaves blew off trees, rivers and lakes turned into ice, and the white smoke that blew from Winter Spirit's mouth turned into snow that fell upon the ground like a white furred rabbit. As Winter Spirit shouted again and again, his breath stirred the snows into raging blizzards. No one answered him.

To see birds and animals squawk and fly away in panic, humans shiver and waters turn to ice was magic and amusing. Winter Spirit did no more than shout to blanch and freeze everything, a winter playground. He followed the birds who flew south to escape his icy breath. It was a game.

Except for the brant, the jay and the raven and a few of their intrepid kin, no one would or could stand up to Winter Spirit. Only the brant dared him to do worse.

Winter Spirit tried, but he couldn't cow or force the brant to give in. It was he who gave up in exasperation.

Leaving the brant be, Winter Spirit resumed his venture further south. By now the game was losing some of its appeal, and was becoming hum-drum.

One morning Winter Spirit woke up drenched from head to foot with sweat. He was warm as if he had a fever, though never having been sick, he didn't know what a fever felt like. He went outside his snowhouse to cool off.

So bright was the sun that Winter Spirit squinted to adjust his vision. When he was able to focus his eyes, Winter Spirit fixed his gaze on a little girl sitting on a snow covered log. Around her head was wound a coronet of roses. Her dress and her moccasins were made of white buckskin.

"Who are you?"

"I'm Zeegwun, Summer Maker's daughter."

"And what are you doing around here?"

"Nothing . . . just walking around. Why?" she explained and asked as if she shouldn't be there.

"Do you know who I am?"

"No! Who are you?" Zeegwun asked innocently, and in such a way as would any child who meets a stranger for the first time—just another way of expressing "am I supposed to?"

"I am Winter Maker! Some people have begun calling me Winter Spirit."

"And what do you do?" Zeegwun asked, not really wanting to know but giving the answer that adults expect.

"You don't know?" Winter Maker roared, put out a little by Zeegwun's lack of fear and knowing nothing about him. He told her, "I can create winds and chill the air so cold that trees shed their leaves, drive bears into the ground, scatter birds before me and cover the earth with snow! And what can you do, if anything?" Winter Maker wanted to know.

"Not very much," Zeegwun answered in a breath soft and sweet such as Winter Maker had never heard. "I'm still too small but I want to be like my mother when I grow up." Around her the snow began to melt. Winter Maker mopped his brow and his neck. "I want the bluebirds and the robins to warble. I want the flowers to grow at my feet and the rain to fall and the wavelets to sparkle." As she prattled on, birds chirped and warbled in the trees, the snow melted even further, the sun shone more brightly, flowers sprang to life, and rain fell.

Winter Maker shrunk smaller and smaller.

"You're crying. You're getting all wet! And you're getting smaller!" Zeegwun whispered in alarm and astonishment. Silently Zeegwun watched Winter Maker shrink and melt away until only a puddle of water remained where he had been standing.

"Poor Winter Maker," Zeegwun sighed, mystified by Winter

Maker's disappearance.

Eight months later Winter Maker's son came back from the Land of Spirits and drove Neebin, which is what Zeegwun had become, back to the South.

And that is how the annual struggle between summer and winter began; between the season of plenty and scarcity.

That was the beginning of the division of time into seasons, and the seasons into months and months into 28 day periods.

There is another explanation for time and the seasons.

When the sky exploded, the earth, the sun and the moon were flung together in the same neighbourhood in the sky, where gravity bound them as neighbours. The earth revolved around the sun, and the moon around the earth. As the earth revolves around the sun, not in a circle but in a parabola, at the same time it revolves around the sun. The earth spins on its axis, it tilts. When the earth is at its furthest distance from the sun and is tilted a few degrees from the sun rays and heat, as if it was leaning back, it is winter. And when the earth is near the sun in its orbit, and is tilted forward, it is summer, with days warmer and longer.

It takes the earth 364.5 days to go around the sun. This period of time is known as "a year." In the western world the year was divided into 12 months. In this system some months had 30 days, others 31, while poor February was short-changed, given only 28 days, and every four years 29. If February weren't given one extra day every fourth year, the man-made calendar would fall behind the true solar time.

The Anishinaubaek, as with most, if not all, North American Indian Nations, had a different system. They divided the year into 13 months of 28 days each, corresponding to the number of times the moon revolved around the earth while the earth revolved once around the sun: $13 \times 28 = 364$.

It is the distance of the earth from the sun and its angle of tilt that influences the seasons and the general climate.

As the earth revolves around the sun and spins on its axis, it disturbs the air around it, causing it to move as wind; its own heat, along with that of the sun and the water, creates clouds or clears the sky of clouds.

Weather, rain, tornado, gale, thunderstorm, cloud, sunshine, winds and their direction, rainlessness, snow, sleet, hail, prolonged cold, sudden warm spells, snowless winters all made some change in the growth of plants and the harvest, which in turn altered and had a bearing upon the habits and the movement of birds, animals, insects and fish.

Whatever weather conditions change the habits of birds and animals and the yield of plants, also change the lives of men and women.

Birds, animals and insects sense the coming changes in the weather and make their own preparations. They tell each other of what they foresee.

Fishermen, hunters and herbalists watch the plants, and listen to birds and animals and insects.

In times past, every evening someone was sure to check aloft and study the clouds and the sun and the direction of the wind and the call of birds.

"Ahneen ae-inaubindukawaeyin?" someone was sure to ask.

And just as surely there was someone who would be scanning the skies at night to see what the stars, northern lights, comets and shooting stars portended as to what the weather would be like in the months to come. It is doubtful that any people were more talented than the Maya in Central America in reading the heavenly bodies. They were able to

calculate the solar year to within a few seconds of its length, and to plot, calculate, and predict eclipses. They developed two numbering systems and a calendric system that meshed, that blended the 13 month and the 20 month neatly together: 13 x 28 = 364; 20 x 18.2 = 364.

The Mayans were able to accomplish their calculations without instruments, using instead their attuned faculties of observation and logic.

READING THE SKY

Sparrow Hawk, a little boy, began his study of the stars when he was five. Except that he didn't know that he was being trained. His grandmother took him out as company and to pass on what she knew about.

"What are you looking at, N'oko?" Sparrow Hawk asked his grandmother on the first night that he stood beside her, after his neck got a kink from tilting his head back.

"Babies," she answered matter-of-factly.

"Babies!" Sparrow Hawk repeated. He looked up again, trying to find even one baby among the countless sparks twinkling in the sky. But he didn't see any, and not seeing any, asked "Where?"

"Up there. They're all over. Little lights, little sparks. See them? They're called stars."

Sparrow Hawk could only gape. He couldn't take in his grand-mother's words. So many babies.

His grandmother went on. "When you were a little star, that's where you were," she explained, pointing to a place in the star world. She continued, telling Sparrow Hawk where she, his grandfather, mother, father, brothers and sisters came from in the sky before they came to the earth.

Sparrow Hawk tried to grasp the incomprehensible in his little head.

Some time later, Sparrow Hawk saw a star fall. He gasped, his voice thin in anxiety. "A baby's falling, N'oko. It's coming down too fast; it's going to get hurt."

"Don't worry grandson. It won't get hurt. It will settle down as gently as a little bird as it alights in its nest. It's a gift. Someone is receiving a gift" and, turning to Sparrow Hawk, added "If ever a star falls near you, take it. Take it home. Look after it and it will bring you many other gifts."

From that night on Sparrow Hawk kept his gaze fixed in the sky, hoping that a star baby would fall nearby. He would take it home to his parents. He would have a brother to play with, or maybe a sister. But no star baby ever fell nearby; the star babies that fell always were far away, gifts for others but not for him. And it made him very sad.

By the time that he was seven, Sparrow Hawk was tired of watching stars; they never changed. None ever fell nearby. And besides, he was beginning to doubt that the so-called "anungook" were babies disguised as stars. To avoid star gazing, Sparrow Hawk invented all kinds of excuses to stay indoors or do something else. Feeling guilty about his loss of interest in stars, Sparrow Hawk accompanied his grandmother once in a while to ease his conscience.

"Why do you keep looking at the stars?" Sparrow Hawk asked his grandmother one evening. He asked this question more to have a good reason to stop star-gazing so that he could do more interesting things with the time saved.

"I watch them because they show me what it's going to be like in the next day or so, whether it's going to storm or it's going to be fair. They also show me what it's going to be like for the next six months, a year; and they show me things that I don't know and make me wonder."

"Why'd you want to know what the weather is going to be like?" Sparrow Hawk broke in, challenging his grandmother to give him a good reason for watching the skies.

"So that you won't be caught out in the lake by a sudden storm, that's why. You want to know ahead of time what it's going to be like. But you have to listen to the stars, the sun, the moon, the northern lights. If you don't pay attention to the signs, you're going to suffer an accident. The Water Manitous will pull you down."

"How can stars know? And the sun? the moon?" Sparrow Hawk asked, doubtful and suspicious that his grandmother was putting him on.

"They are friends, our friends. They do favours for us."

"How? Why?" he remarked, skeptical.

Sparrow Hawk's grandmother told him the following story.

THE BEAR, THE LITTLE BEAR, AND THE FISHER

A long time ago bears, giant bears, used to hunt human beings, who lived in constant terror for their lives. Years went by before Kitchi-Manitou took pity on human beings by punishing the Giant Bears. Kitchi-Manitou put a curse on the Giant Bears. Instantly the Giant Bears were stricken in size. They grew smaller and smaller until they became no bigger than dwarfs compared to what they were. Kitchi-Manitou also took away their ferocity. The Giant Bears were transformed into squirrels, red, black, gray, and flying; so timid that they constantly shiver and tremble. When the dwarf creatures realized what happened, they fled into tall trees.

The squirrels were in constant dread of little boys and hawks. There was not a moment during the day when they could relax. They were tense, ready to dive for cover and hide. Other birds and animals preyed on them and looked upon them as little cowards. More than anything else they wanted to get over this feeling that something was about to happen or that someone was about to do them in. Now they felt as if they knew what humans must have gone through when they were hunted, never to know peace of mind. They thought that if they could do something for human beings they would get some peace of mind and spirit.

The chance didn't come until much later. And it came because Winter Maker's pride was wounded by his being bested by a little girl. He wouldn't have minded too much if it had been a man forcing him to give in. But a little girl!

Winter Maker had a friend living in the south. He sent a message asking his friend to capture the little girl and to keep her prisoner somewhere, maybe in a cave. His friend, a southern bear, had no trouble catching Zeegwun and holding her captive in a cave.

Up north the Anishinaubae peoples and their neighbours and the animals waited for Zeegwun. She was late and there was no sign of her coming. Food was running low. If she didn't arrive soon, people would dig for roots to eat.

"Where is Zeegwun?" the squirrels asked, and their questions echoed across the tree tops all the way to the south.

A squirrel who had seen the kidnapping of Zeegwun knew where the little girl was hidden. As a southern dweller, the squirrel didn't know why the little girl was so important to the northern inhabitants.

When he learned that the little girl beat back Winter Maker and brought life back to the plants and made the birds chirp and warble in cheerfulness, the little squirrel watched the entrance to the cave.

So sure were the guards that their prisoner wouldn't get out and run off that they slept. While the guards were sleeping the squirrel slipped by them and opened the door. The moment the door was open, Zeegwun escaped.

The guards woke up. Too late. Zeegwun was gone.

Nearby, up in the tree, thinking that the guards would not suspect or see him, was the little squirrel. Close by was a fisher minding his business doing what fishers do.

The chief guardian of Zeegwun had been a large white bear, an albino. Without waiting to ask questions, he and his followers unleashed a hail of angry words and arrows at the little squirrel and the startled fisher.

Both the squirrel and the fisher turned tail and ran for their lives up a mountain. Behind them the albino bear and his followers were closing in fast, firing arrow after arrow. The little squirrel and the fisher leaped into the sky. The albino bear also leaped into the sky.

On the mountain top the albino bear's followers fired arrows like lightning bolts at the little squirrel and the fisher. They couldn't miss. They hit their targets, pinning both of them to the sky. But they also hit their own leader, pinning him to the sky as well.

Frightened by what they had done to their chief, the followers ran off, leaving the albino bear, the little squirrel and the fisher in a strange world among strangers.

The strangers, star people, asked them what they were doing in a world where they didn't belong. After the little squirrel finished his explanation, telling how he meant to do humans a good deed to make up for the wrongs that he and his kin had done, he asked the star people to let him go so that he could do something worthwhile. As for the fisher who'd had nothing to do with the quarrel between the albino bear and the little squirrel, he asked to be sent back home. The albino bear demanded to be released and sent back to earth at once.

"No," the star-people could not set them free.

"Then, how can I do something that would be useful to the earth beings from up here? What would he like to do? They need to know what the weather is going to be like and that spring will never be held up too long."

"We will make signs to let them know that we are changing the weather."

THE SIGNS

At night the star beings come out and light up the sky as so many tiny sparks: red, blue, green, pink, white. They flicker and glow, spin and quiver, dance and hold still. They streak across the sky like rockets or fall like hail and shower the heavens. Northern lights (aurora borealis) that glow, green, pink, blue and white and flare up and flash down, backward and forward, are made by the fires set by the souls and spirits of the dead as they pass along the chilly Path of Souls, the milky way. The star beings create fireworks every night. These are signs that only the experienced can read.

Some signs are easy to read. Every grown person once knew what they were.

If Father Sun's face is bright, red or yellow (gold), glowing in good humour as it settles down for the night, the next day will be fair, sunny and warm.

On the other hand, if the sun draws a grey blanket of clouds over his face and rays flare out from behind the clouds as it turns in for the night, the day following will be unsettled for certain, stormy with thunder and lightning, maybe just rainy.

But the sun and the moon give at least three days' warning that inclement weather is on its way. A halo around the sun is a sign of bad weather. In summer it means that a storm, thunder and lightning are in the making. At the same time the days are hot and humid. In winter the ring signifies a snowstorm, hail, freezing rain, a blizzard, or just plain rain.

When our ancestors saw the halo they used to say that "Father Sun is going into his wigwaum to take shelter from the rain or from the coming snows." He's showing human beings that thunders and lightnings, snows and cold are being stirred up. At night, Grandmother Moon gives similar signs.

Now and then in winter Father Sun is flanked by two bright bars on each side as it sets down for the night. At other times there is but a single bar of light directly over it. Of these signs our ancestors used to say "Father Sun is making two fires. It's going to be frosty biting cold." Or in the case of a single bright bar, "Father Sun is making an extra warm fire. It's going to be tree crackling cold."

Our ancestors paid attention to these warnings.

Birds, animals and insects know and heed these signs better than do humans, not only weather signs but the seasonal change signs. Watch our neighbours, meaning the birds, the animals and the insects. Listen to them. They know better than human beings what changes are in the air. How do birds, animals and insects know? Who knows? They just know. They sense and they know. Maybe they sense barometric and atmospheric changes in a way that a human senses hunger for a particular kind of food.

When owls were created, Kitchi-Manitou assigned them to be lookouts for humans, animals, birds and insects, and to give warning of changes in the weather, especially thunder storms and blizzards. With big eyes that could see in the dark as well as in the day, owls could see three to four days ahead of a storm, and talk about it among themselves. Weather was all that owls talked about. "Big storm on the way; last maybe two or three days, lots of rain. Pass it on." And they'd pass it on to other owls. In no time, even before the night was over, owls three days away would know about the forthcoming storm. So would everybody else.

Owls are not much different from anybody else who keeps watch. There were no great storms, and the ones that rolled over the land were tame, the kind that no one needed to be concerned with. They were hardly worth the bother of staying awake for all night, and then sitting around the next day only half awake from lack of sleep.

With next to nothing to do, the owls took to stealing longer naps, taking 80 winks rather than 40. Nobody suffered any harm; no one was aware that the night watchmen were sleeping on the job.

When the first drops of rain that flooded the world began to fall, the owls woke up too late to issue timely warnings to the living world. It was late, too late, but the owls hooted nevertheless, more to show that they were doing what they were supposed to be doing, but they too, along with the rest of the living world, were caught napping.

They were a mighty wretched flock of guilty-looking owls perched on branches and stumps that floated about in the floodwaters, waiting for the end.

Nana'b'oozoo didn't waste any time in punishing the owls after he and the other living creatures were once more safe on land. He twisted their necks, meaning to pull their heads off but he took pity on them, so loudly did they cry for their lives and for another chance. Besides, there were others, owls' kin and friends, who growled "leave them alone; they didn't do it on purpose." But Nana'b'oozoo gave the owls a stern warning not to fall asleep again on the job. Otherwise he'd pull their heads right off.

Not wanting to have their heads pulled off, the owls returned to their lookouts, their big eyes wide open to look at the stars by night and to study the clouds and the atmosphere by day. Their ears too are keen to take in the most tiny and distant sounds. If they hear a worm cough 10 miles away behind them, owls can turn their heads completely around without having to turn their bodies, and fix their gaze upon the offending worm until the worm stops coughing.

As good as most other birds, animals and insects, and maybe better, owls sense the beat of Mother Earth's heart. They can sense her thirst, her longing for cleansing. And they can sense the thunderbirds stirring to build thunderbird fires that make thunderfire smoke called clouds, filled with rain. When owls sense, three to four days beforehand, that the thunderbirds are about to let the rains loose, they let the whole world know. They don't hoot, as some people believe; they only sound as if they are hooting. They are talking in their own language: "Mother Earth needs rain, the plants need rain" they all agree. "Hope the thunderbirds don't overdo the watering and flood the earth as they once did ages ago."

Word that rain is on its way rouses everybody. They don't want to be caught unprepared as they were once caught off guard. Mosquitoes, blackflies, horse flies, deer flies, house flies, long remembering how many of their ancestors starved to death and drowned, hearing the owls announce that a storm is due to break within the next few days, gorge themselves on blood, the blood of humans and animals. They bug human beings. Nowadays they get blamed for ruining week-ends.

Owls aren't the only birds to warn people of impending storms. Nighthawks, usually quiet, leave their nests and take to the air, circling and dipsy-doodling, dipping and diving like dancers. At the bottom of a dip they burp, sounding as if they had strep throat. Actually, they aren't dancing, they are eating, eating as many flying insects as they can, and as fast as they can. And, because they bolt their food alive, nighthawks belch.

Owls and nighthawks warn each other and the living world of coming storms, and maybe the kind and its duration, but human beings don't know enough of owl and nighthawk language to understand.

KINDS OF WEATHER

TORNADOES — In Anishinaubae country the worst kind of summer storm that can strike is the tornado which, fortunately, does not occur as often or with as much force as it does in the south. Run, hide, find a cave, a hollowed depression, and hope and pray. A black clouded tornado is like some great dark bird, drifting slowly along low in the sky, with its great beak probing and sweeping the earth for food and drink to quell and quench its gigantic hunger and thirst. As it sweeps over the land, it rips and uproots trees, pitches them to one side, whips the lakes into boiling fury and whirling masses.

This dark mass of cloud, with a funnel pointed to the earth, is a ghost of a little bird, a little sparrow.

As a nestling, the little sparrow listened to its mother tell stories about thunderbirds and eagles and other birds. From the day the little sparrow saw eagles for the first time it wanted to be an eagle, not just an ordinary, common sparrow. It wanted to fly high, above the clouds.

Mother Sparrow told her offspring that sparrows were not meant to fly with eagles; they were too small to ride the updrafts, to float on them. Still, the little sparrow dreamed.

When the little sparrow was able, it used to fly out of its mother's sight to play, pretending to be an eagle. It would find the updrafts that seagulls float on and ride them. Invisible waves he called them. It was exciting to mount and ride an updraft that rose and fell like a wave. If an updraft took him up too fast, the little sparrow jumped off and, breathless, flew home.

But the little sparrow played this game once too often. It hitched a ride on a raft of air that carried it so swiftly that the little sparrow was afraid to jump off. Higher and higher the cushion of air carried the little sparrow.

Frightened, the little sparrow cried out for its mother, but its cry was no louder or stronger than a mouse's squeak, and easily drowned out by the winds. It cried out until its throat was parched. It needed to drink. It was hungry and needed to eat. But where the little sparrow was, there was nothing to eat or drink.

The little sparrow looked down from the edge of a great cloud. Far below was its home with all the water that it would ever want. The earth spun around. The little sparrow closed its eyes and opened its beak as it used to do for its mother.

Down below the water manitous, feeling sorry for the little spar-row, allowed some water to be drawn into the sky, into the sparrow's throat. The sparrow drank and it drank. With each swallow it got bigger and bigger, but it didn't know of its growth in size. The cushion of air hidden behind a large cloud was carried along by strong winds so that the sparrow, now a giant bird, drew up and pulled up everything in its path like a suction pump.

In its path the tornado wrought havoc and destruction. Birds, ani-mals and human beings, seeing it come, hid wherever they could find shelter. They prayed.

THUNDER STORMS — Kitchi-Manitou created Thunderbirds to look after Mother Earth's needs by providing her with water to refresh and to cleanse her; to keep the lakes full and the forests clean. In caring for Mother Earth, they storm and thunder around in the sky, stirring up winds and dust that turns into clouds. Their eyes flash lightning and fire-bolts of flaming arrows at the earth as they open the floodgates in the sky. The Anishinaubae peoples offered tobacco to the thunderbirds before the storm as a way of asking them to be sparing in watering the earth and not to unleash too many Thunderbolts. And, after a storm passed, our ancestors offered tobacco in thanksgiving for the life-giving, cleansing rain.

The scientific explanation differs from that of our ancestors. Climatologists say lightning is caused by electric charges unleashed from cloud to cloud or from cloud to earth. The release of an electric charge is followed by an explosion that climatologists and everybody calls thunder.

To make sure that his student understood thunderstorms and their causes without referring to scientific terms such as barometric pres-sure, isobars, celsius, cold and warm fronts, a certain teacher chose to use hot and cold air mass. "When these collide, crash together as it were, they cause lightning and thunder."

The students accepted this explanation without question. The teacher's word was incontestable. Besides, it was written down in a book.

This kind of revelation is just the kind that 14 year old students latch onto to show that they know something that their parents don't know, especially if their parents had no formal education. Then they could set their parents straight.

After one violent thunderstorm a student so newly instructed in grade 9 climatology, straightened out his father who had offered thanksgiving to the Thunderbirds. The boy told him about hot and cold fronts crashing and producing clouds, thunder and lightning. There were no such things as Thunderbirds. Besides, offering tobacco and praying to Thunderbirds was a sin, pagan. His father could go to hell for that. Almost as bad, White People would laugh at him for believing in fairy tales.

The boy's father was ashamed. He didn't want the White People, who knew everything, to laugh at him. Neither did he want to go to hell. He put Thunderbirds out of his mind, but he couldn't accept the crashing of hot and cold air with sufficient force to provide fireworks and explosions in the sky. Pretty soft stuff ... air.

At home the following winter, in the warmth of his house and numbing cold outside, the father's mind began to dabble with the White Man's explanation for the cause of storms. Outdoor fires in winter didn't anger the heavens. Cold air in summer. It was chilly sometimes, but not cold. Maybe the hot air must be hotter than hot.

How was he to find out if hot air crashing into cold caused lightning and thunder as the White Man said. Only by experimenting, the White Man's way. And there was no better time than now, with the temperature 38° below outside.

He fired his stove with cedar kindling and oak. Soon he was dripping sweat down his face. His wife Margaretwas barking at him, "What're you trying to do? Burn the house down?"

"No! I'm making experiment like White Man's. Find out that hot air and cole air make thunner and lightning."

"Why don't you let White Mans make his own experi-ment?"

31

"I'm goin' to open that door afore I strangles to de't."

"No! No! Not yit. Jist wait couple more minutes. Den I'll open it."

His wife, wiping her face with a handkerchief, waited, muttering about "mins and White Mins wedder-mans hardly gits the wedder right half de times. My art-rightus was better den all dem bulloons and contraptions White Mans use."

"Okay! Maugneet. Get ready."

"About times!" Margaret growled.

"You should go upstairs. Cover up your ears. Never know what's gone happen when liddle bit o' hot air crash wit' col' air outside."

Margaret stood where she was, hands on her hips.

Max turned the latch and yanked the door open toward him. He closed his eyes expectantly. There was no explosion. Then he opened them slowly.

"Close de door! Bullhead!" Maugneet sneered. And, seeing the door knob in her husband's hand, added "Guess de lightning bolt musta blow dat knobs right off."

Only then did Max notice that he had pulled the latch off its mount.

WINDS — The air is seldom still. It may never be still, for that matter. Even on a calm day when the lake's surface is like a mirror, or a still cold winter's night when trees crackle, there is motion in the air. Leaves move, grass bends, snowflakes move as if caressed by some invisible hand. At other times the wind is balmy, soft as a baby's breath or it roars and shrieks as it tears along bending trees, even breaking their limbs, and whipping the waves into froth and mist. In winter it will drive snow from the ground into blizzards so thick that neither man nor animals can see or hear.

"What is that?" every child wants to know when he or she hears the moan of the wind for the first time.

"It's only the wind."

"What's the wind? Where is it? I can't see it."

"It's nothing to be afraid of. It won't hurt you. Just remember that Nana'b'oozoo and Pukawiss are chasing each other so fast that they stir up the air and everything. They are playing."

"Can I see them?"

"No you can't. They're invisible."

"But how can they see each other if they're invisible?"

"Because they're manitous."

"And they play?"

"Yes and no. Not always. Only when Pukawiss does something to Nana'b'oozoo, which is most of the time. For Pukawiss it's a game, but for Nana'b'oozoo it's not a game. Pukawiss likes to tease Nana'b'oozoo because his younger brother can't take a joke. He's got such a short temper. And so Pukawiss teases Nana'b'oozoo to goad him.

It all began a long time ago.

Nana'b'oozoo had a flock of white pigeons. He cared more for these pigeons than anyone or anything else in the world. Every evening he took his pigeons down to the lake where he washed them until they were glistening white. He even took them into the house. When he went away during the day he made his grandmother care for the pigeons.

Nana'b'oozoo wasn't home one day when Pukawiss came over to visit him. It was then that their grandmother told Pukawiss how much work she had to do to care for Nana'b'oozoo's pigeons. They could look after themselves.

For Nana'b'oozoo to make their grandmother work wasn't right. He needed to be taught a lesson. Pukawiss made pitch which he coated on the pigeons. While he was painting the pigeons, his grandmother pleaded with him not to do it. 'Nana'b'oozoo will make me clean the pigeons.'

'Noko! Don't worry' Pukawiss assured his grandmother. 'I won't let him do anything to you.'

When Nana'b'oozoo got home that evening, the first thing that he did was to inspect his pigeons. Tonight, instead of crooning, 'Kissy!

Kissy! Say Ahneeeee!' as he entered the coop, Nana'b'oozoo roared 'Who's done this? I'll wring his neck! NOKO! Weren't you watching my birds as you were supposed to?' he demanded.

From his hiding spot in the nearby woods, unseen in the dark, Pukawiss cackled through his nose in derision. Nana'b'oozoo yelled out at his brother, 'Wait till I get my hands on you tomorrow. You'll be chanting your death chant.' Pukawiss cackled again.

In the morning, when Nana'b'oozoo finished cleaning his birds, he left them in the care of his grandmother. Then, club in hand, he tore into the woods to crack Pukawiss's skull open.

Pukawiss bolted away like a deer, his brother right behind. They raced across meadows, above tree tops, up hills, down valleys, over the waves. They back-tracked, they zig-zagged, they ran in circles. They slowed down as if to pace themselves, and then turned on the jets. When they reduced their pace, the only sign of the invisible race was the rustle of leaves, the combing of grasses, the ripples on the water, the shifting of snow. At the height of their speed, the jet stream behind ripped leaves off trees, branches off limbs, raised whirlwinds, twisted water into spouts and snow into dancing twisters.

And if Nana'b'oozoo broke off chasing him, Pukawiss would do something to provoke his younger brother to take up the chase and run once again. Teasing, making fun of people and manitous who took them-selves too seriously provided Pukawiss with all the amusement that he needed. And Nana'b'oozoo was as easily provoked as any human being, ready to drop whatever he was doing to uphold his reputation and his sense of honour.

Nana'b'oozoo gave up hope of getting his hands on his brother Pukawiss. He had a good excuse. Parents needed him to persuade their children to eat vegetables and nuts that were good for them.

Children turned away from carrots, turnips, peas, pumpkins. They pretended to gag on cucumbers and cabbage. Nothing, not the promise of maple sugar or honey could make them eat morels, leeks, rhubarb.

At least not until Nana'b'oozoo dabbed some colour on vegetables, fruits and nuts; sprayed them with perfume and put pleasant flavours in each did children help themselves to eat what was good for them without argument.

To do what he did for children pleased Nana'b'oozoo. He was proud of what he had done, and tired to his very bones. He collapsed on his pallet.

In the morning Nana'b'oozoo was awakened by voices calling him and saying 'Someone's bleached everything; all the apples, flowers are white, pale as ghosts.'

Nana'b'oozoo, eyes half closed, went outside. He blinked. It was true. Everything was white. Something had happened, someone had discoloured everything.

Still tired, Nana'b'oozoo went to work to restore the colours to vegetables, fruits, and nuts. As he darted from cucumbers to apples, to acorns, dyeing them again, someone laughed at him from behind. 'Heeee! Heee! Haaa! Nana'b'oozoo! You should take a rest now and then. You must get tired from overwork.' The laugh and the words burned Nana'b'oozoo's ears.

While Nana'b'oozoo was re-dyeing everything, a cicada came out of the ground where it had spent 17 years in the first part of its life. It was dazzled by the bright sunlight that it had never seen, and dazed.

'Who are you? What do you do?' Nana'b'oozoo asked.

'I don't know. I've never been here!' the cicada answered.

'Would you like to do something? For me?' Nana'b'oozoo asked. 'Something easy. Like painting vegetables, fruits and nuts while I go for a while. I've got something to do. I'll come right back and you can do whatever you want.'

'Be glad to' the cicada obliged.

The cicada started at once, beating its wings to brush the dye on everything. Wanting to do the job properly, it dyed everything: leaves, grasses, hay, flowers.

As soon as the cicada started dyeing, Nana'b'oozoo raced off to catch Pukawiss. Almost immediately he forgot the cicada, whose descendants inherited the job of dyeing all plants, and still do that to the present day. So hard do they dye for Nana'b'oozoo that they work themselves to an early death, living above ground no longer than six weeks."

PLANTS

Every spring a miracle takes place in the land of the Anishinaubaek. The snow melts under the warm rays of the sun that has drawn the earth closer to it in its orbit. Zeegwun is wearing down Abiboon. Even before all the snow melts and there is still a thin layer on the ground, little green shoots and blades of grass break through the cold hard cover.

Within weeks after the snow is melted the forest floor and the countryside are ablaze with flowers of every kind. The woodlands and the meadows look as if the flowers had spilled down from the sky. On the trees are blossoms, apple, cherry, pear, peach, lilac.

Sweet and delicate scents of millions of flowers and blossoms aromate the air. Bees and their kin awaken from their winter sleep to the fragrances that fill the air. They are hungry, hungry for the sweet nectar that each flower bears.

First, little white and blue flowers, then yellow ones, violets, arbutuses, dogtooth violets, dandelions, trilliums, lady's slippers, cherry blossoms, apple blossoms, lilacs. They unfold their petals, glow in hundreds of different hues, scent the air with fragrances unnamed, then fade and change. Their life span, with the exception of a few species, is maybe at most three weeks. So short the season, so short life.

In three weeks the blossoms' colours fade and its blossoms fall apart petal by petal, and the heart of the flower becomes hard and takes the form of an apple or a strawberry, or a tomato. Another miracle has taken place.

Children, bringing flowers to their mothers as presents, asked and still ask, "Where do flowers come from?

Did they fall from the sky as the old people used to say, or did they all come from little seeds? And where did the little seeds come from?"

But the old people had only one story.

Flowers are star children, sons and daughters of Grandfather Sun and Grandmother Moon. The star children slept all day, coming out only at night to play. They were allowed to play any game they wanted, anywhere they wanted in the sky, while Grandfather Sun was at work providing light and warmth to the earth. There was only one rule that they had to obey and that is, they had to be home and abed before dawn every day, before Grandfather Sun came home. Just before dawn every day the star children streaked home, dove into their beds, and settled down to sleep.

But one night several star children came down to earth to play. At first they kept their chatter and laughter in check. However, before long they were squealing and thumping around as they bounced along the treetops and on top of the water. The star children created such a din that they awakened a boy and his sister, who caught them and locked them up in a box.

From the moment of their capture the star children cried "We want to go home! Grandfather Sun and Grandmother Moon will punish us. Please let us go home."

Crying and begging didn't do the star children any good. The boy and girl wouldn't let them go. They wanted to keep them as pets.

All day the star children cried, afraid that Grandfather Sun would learn where they were. Then he would come for them and punish them for not going home by burning them up.

When Grandfather Sun took his light home and left the earth in darkness, the little star children lit their little lights in their little prison. As soon as it was dark the Earth children opened the box to play with the new toys, but the star children refused to leave the box. They begged and begged to be allowed to go home.

Only after the Earth children promised to let them go home did the star children play. As an extra reward, the star children promised to send gifts to the Earth children when they got home to their Sky World.

In the morning the boy and his sister, and every other boy and girl in the Earth World, found millions and billions of brightly coloured plants, bees and tiny little insects looking after the pretty, sweet smelling crowns. The Earth people called them "wauwauss-konae" meaning "brightly clad" or little lights that brighten. There is perhaps no better word for these crownlets.

The little boy and the little girl picked dandelions and daisies and lilies for their mother as a sign of their love. To this day children pick flowers and give them to their mothers. Men buy roses for their sweet-hearts. Painters have drawn flowers, and poets have written about them.

Flowers are beautiful. They are many things. They are the garments of Mother Earth. In the spring they come to life, live out their span of life in three weeks, and are no more. Poets lament how short-lived is the flower, how beauty soon fades. But flowers exist not only to please the eye. After the last petal of each flower fades and falls, another miracle in life takes place. The matrix changes and turns into an apple, pear, peach, berry, tomato, cucumber. The plant's stem, leaves and roots become medicine, Mashki-Aki, strength of the earth.

PLANTS AS FOOD

CORN — Corn, one of the four principal foods in the world, along with potatoes, rice and wheat, was developed by the Toltec Indians in Mexico, near what is now Mexico City. So far as is known, corn is the only food developed by man, and is the only one completely dependent upon humans for its growth to maturity. "Maundau-meen" is known to the Anishinaubae peoples and other North American Indians as an immigrant, a plant not native to this part of the world. Still, it is welcome and has been long a mainstay in the diet of our ancestors.

Maundau-meen arrived as a stranger in Anishinaubae country. In fact, its coming was foretold by an aged grandmother just before she passed away. "A stranger will come. Listen to him" the grandmother had told her grandson, Zhoowi-meen.

"I will," Zhoowi-meen promised his grandmother.

For sure, a stranger arrived in Zhoowi-meen's village the spring following his grandmother's death. Impressive he was, taller than most of the men in the village. His clothing too caught the eye, his vest, leggings and loincloth were green, and his headdress was made of a fine brown tassel that hung down to his shoulders.

Zhoowi-meen's neighbours asked the stranger where he came from and what he was doing in Anishinaubae land. To their surprise the stranger answered in the Anishinaubae language, telling them that he came from a land far to the south, and that he was looking for someone to stand up to him. He wanted to see what stuff the Anishinaubae people were made of. If any man or woman could put him down, the victor's life would be richer; if not, the vanquished warrior's people would never know or see change.

The Anishinaubaek didn't understand what the stranger meant, and didn't really care. Their lives were already rich enough. But what made them bristle was the stranger's hint that if they didn't accept his challenge, he would take it as a sign of weakness.

"You!" the stranger said, looking at Zhoowi-meen.

With every eye upon him, Zhoowi-meen squirmed. In size he was no match for the stranger. He looked for a way out, but he didn't want to be thought of as cowardly. Then he remembered his grandmother's words.

"Yes!" he said to save face.

For four days Zhoowi-meen and the nameless stranger fought. On the fourth night, Zhoowi-meen struck a lucky blow. The stranger was dead by the time he hit the ground.

Zhoowi-meen was horrified by what he'd done, but it was either him or the stranger. But some of his neighbours gloated, "serves him right. Let's see what good he'll do us! Let's see if he's as good as his word."

Zhoowi-meen and the people of his village buried the rash foreign warrior next to his grandmother's grave. Whenever Zhoowi-meen came to pay his respects to his grandmother, he paid his respects to the nameless stranger as well.

In early June, Zhoowi-meen noticed a plant, such as he had never before seen in his part of the world, growing on top of the stranger's grave. Odd, he thought. During the weeks that followed the more pronounced was the difference between the new plant and the others. No one, not even the members of the Medaewaewin, a medicine society, could say what the plant was.

"Keep an eye on it," was the only advice they gave.

Two months later, during the raspberry month now called August, the medicine people sampled the yellow kernels of this strange plant, and declared them to be good. "Maundau-meen" they called the new plant, a seed or berry of wonder. A more fitting name could not have been coined for this plant that had been transmitted from its native home in Central Mexico through trade from nation to nation. And as it was adopted by people, maundau-meen changed the way of life for most people. Some gave up hunting to till the land. Most blended hunting and tilling the land as a way of life and providing sustenance for their families.

In trading for corn, our ancestors also learned how to grow and care for corn.

At first people took care of their gift of corn as great gifts are supposed to be treasured. It had made their lives just a little easier. But soon they were taking corn for granted. There was corn aplenty, enough for mice, crows, ravens, blue jays, raccoons, insects and humans. Men and women grew more than they needed, they cooked more than they could eat. They ate only the choice parts, throwing out what they regarded as worthless to their dogs, or just casting it aside for maggots. There was so much corn; no need to husband it.

But the harvests of corn dwindled little by little so that people didn't notice what was taking place and, if they did, didn't give it a second thought. It was only years later that people awakened to the dwindling crops.

"There was a lot more corn years ago," they reminded each other and their children.

"Don't worry," they answered each other. "Happens once in a while. Just wait! Cornfields will be as fruitful as before. You'll see!"

The people tended their corn and fields with even greater care, but the crops dwindled even further. There was not enough to keep families fed for a while winter. So much work, so little reward.

Finally the old people gathered together to discuss the crop shortages of corn. They agreed that someone or all of them had done something to offend the Spirit of Corn. To learn why the Spirit of Corn was punishing the people, the elders appointed their wisest person to speak to the Spirit of Corn and to learn why corn was getting ever leaner and thinner.

The Spirit of Corn answered that men and women didn't deserve corn as food to keep them alive and in good health. People wasted corn, they gave it to their dogs as unwanted left-overs. Corn had come to have no meaning to the people than worm eaten apples. But if people were to mend their ways and to give corn the respect that it deserves, the Spirit would restore corn to the fields in quantity to keep people well fed.

The wise man came back with the Spirit of Corn's message. That same day the people performed a pow-wow in thanksgiving for all past harvests, and promised that in the future they would bury or burn the husks or make something useful from them as a mark of respect. From then on the corn planters offered tobacco when they planted the kernels, and again when they harvested the crops.

WILD RICE — MINO-MEEN --- Nana'b'oozoo was required to seek a dream, like everyone else. Many times he tried, but he was never able to fast for four entire days as everyone seeking a dream or vision was required to do. He could not fight off hunger or thirst. He ate and he drank. He gave in to his belly, which was his master. As a result, Nana'b'oozoo didn't dream.

It wasn't until he was a man that Nana'b'oozoo managed to master his belly for four full days. He collapsed from hunger as he had always feared, and slept. All around him birds flew and chattered. In the back, perched on dead trees, were buzzards waiting to clean up. Nana'b'oozoo woke up with a start. He cried out. Then he managed to fall back to sleep.

At dawn he woke up. Already the birds were squawking and carrying on worse than jays down near the shore. Within range of his bow and arrow loitered deer and rabbits hopped by just beyond reach of his hand. His belly called out "Food! Food!" Nana'b'oozoo tried to stand up, his knees bent and he fell back, weak.

Desperately hungry, Nana'b'oozoo crawled down to the water's edge to drink. From the shore and away grew tall grasses that drooped under the weight of the birds and seeds. The birds were feeding. There was nothing to eat, nothing except this bird food. After he slaked his thirst, Nana'b'oozoo pulled a stock down, took a handful of seed and ate them. He ate and ate until he could eat no more.

After he gorged himself, Nana'b'oozoo fell asleep for several days.

He woke up to an enormous hunger. Nana'b'oozoo was hungry, but not to the point where he'd eat the "bird seed" uncooked. Instead, he boiled the seed in a birch bark container that he made.

At home, Nana'b'oozoo could not persuade his neighbours to eat the "bird seed" as they called it. Only after they'd seen Nana'b'oozoo's grandmother eat the "mino-meen" (the good seed) as she called it, did they try it. From that day, wild rice, as it's called today, became a regular part of the Anishinaubae peoples' diet.

It grew in warm shallow waters from the Kawarthas in Eastern Ontario to the Northern states of Michigan, Wisconsin and Minnesota and on into Northwestern Ontario. To the people in the Northwest, "Mino-meen" was a staple in much the same way as corn was a staple in the south. So much so did one people in Wisconsin depend upon Mino-meen that they were called The Menominee, the good seed people.

The Anishinaubae people called this food "the good seed." It is not a rice as people of West European extraction called it. Rather, it is a grain that grows in water. A good thing that it was not beneath Nana'b'oozoo's dignity to eat what was regarded as bird food.

STRAWBERRIES — Our people called these berries "heart berries" because they are heart-shaped and blood-coloured. They are the first berries to ripen in the spring, in June, which is known as heart berry month. The berries are good to eat and their leaves and roots are medicinal, good for the heart. They came to people in the following way.

A little boy fell into a deep coma, the victim of an epidemic that killed many people. His people and his family cried at his bedside for three days. So long as his parents and his kin cried for him, so long did he in his soul-spirit form linger on earth near his body. When his family had given him up as dead, the little boy as soul-spirit left the earth and walked to the Land of Souls along the Path of Souls.

When he arrived at the Gateway to the Land of Souls the Watcher asked, "What brings you here so soon. You must scarce be seven, no more than eight?"

"It was a sickness. It put us to sleep. I didn't want to leave home. Where am I?"

The Watcher told the little boy where he was, then asked if the little boy had some special request.

"Yes! I want to go home. But if you won't let me go home, will you put a stop to the sickness?"

The Watcher told the little boy to wait, then disappeared. A little later he was back. "We don't want you yet," he said. "We will give you what you want for your people."

The little boy stirred as his family and kin were preparing him for burial. His soul-spirit had re-entered his body. He said that he'd had a dream, that he'd gone as far as the gates to the Land of Souls. The medicine men and women who had attended him said that the boy had experienced delirium.

The boy himself became a medicine man who served his people for many years. When he died berries that looked like little hearts and were as red as blood grew on the mound of the old man's grave. The Anishinaubaek called this berry "Odae-meen," the heart berry.

RASPBERRIES — Before the sun and the moon and the stars were lit, there was no light. The animals, birds, insects and fish were huddled somewhere in the newly-created earth. They crowded so close together than they stepped on each other's feet and elbowed each other in the ribs. There were frequent growls and snarls breaking the air. "Get off my feet! Move over! I can't breathe! You'll crush my box!"

Until this animal mentioned "box" no one knew that others had a box. Each one believed that he was the only one with a gift. Each one cradled his gift close to his side.

When the Bear heard her neighbour utter the word "box," she was surprised. Like everybody else, the Bear believed that she was the only lucky one to have a present.

"I have one too," Bear growled.

"What have you got?" Beaver asked.

"I don't know! I haven't opened my present yet."

"Well, open it."

"No! You first!"

They bickered and snapped at each other as to whom was to be the first to open her present. They shook their boxes near their ears; they held them near their noses to help them learn what was inside. Had it not been for Bear, who grew impatient with her neighbours' nattering "No! You first!" might have gone on and on. The Bear roared for quiet and growled, "I'll open my box first if the rest of you open yours."

Everyone wanted the honour of being next. The dark sounded like a frog pond during a spring night with all the spring peepers chanting "I want to be next."

"Quiet" the bear roared.

The voices died away in a hushed silence.

The Bear opened her present. As she put her paw inside and drew out a small soft object, she tried to describe what she held. "It's small ... soft." She held it to her nose, "smells good." She put it to her mouth. "It is sweet. Mmmm! It's good to eat" she declared.

"What is it?" the crowd wanted to know.

"I'll call it a raspberry," the bear answered.

"Can I have some? Can I have some?" rang and echoed in the dark.

"I'm sorry, but I don't have enough to give one berry to everybody. I wish I had more but I have only so much. I've only got a small box. I've only got enough for a few of you."

There were groans of disappointment from front to back, with the loudest coming from those furthest from the Bear. "We're not going to get any," they grumbled.

But a marvelous, wonderful thing happened that mystified Bear. No matter how often she put her paw into her box to withdraw a berry, the box remained full. Even after the bear had given a berry to every bird, animal, and insect and fish, her box was as full as before.

All the other birds, animals and insects had gifts that were as self-replenishing as the Bear's gift.

Our ancestors considered themselves lucky for the countless gifts that they'd received from Mother Earth and Kitchi-Manitou. Though they were not aware of it, the Anishinaubaek and other American Indians occupied lands in North and South America that yielded a greater variety of foods, fruit, vegetables, nuts, berries and tubers than the rest of the world. It's been said that nearly 60 percent of the world's foods came from the lands of the American Indians.

Famine was unknown. If a man and his family went hungry, it was not because food was lacking; it was because the provider was lazy.

Food was for everyone, humans, birds, animals, insects and fish, for this generation, the next and all those that followed. Mother Earth gave and gave. No matter how much she gave, Mother Earth's breadbasket never gave out.

PLANTS AS MEDICINE

THE WHITE WATER LILY — After the little Sky Watcher heard his grandmother say that falling stars and comets were great gifts sent to people, he watched the stars and prayed that one would fall nearby as a gift meant for him. But no star fell nearby; they all fell far away as gifts for others. He prayed and hoped until he soured on stars and his grandmother.

His grandmother fell ill and was confined to bed. How seriously sick she was, Sky Watcher didn't know. The only inkling that he had that she must be very sick was the coming and going of many kin and medicine people. To Sky Watcher, there was nothing to worry about; his grandmother was indestructible. She would recover.

One evening he went outside and stood on the rock that his grandmother was fond of standing on as she read the skies. It felt strange to stand there alone in his grandmother's place. It was not the same.

He looked up and, as his eyes swept the vast sky, a star fell. It streaked over his head and disappeared beyond a hill that sloped into a large pond on the other side, not far from where he stood. His gift! Sky Watcher sprinted up the hill and down the far side, anxious to claim it before anyone else took possession.

But there was no star on the pond, no shining object, nothing worthwhile taking as a gift except hundreds of white flowers floating on the surface that weren't there before.

Disappointed, he turned away from the pond and the flowers. As he did so a voice called out to him, "Take me. I am medicine. Take me and I will make your grandmother well."

Sky Watcher turned around to see who was calling, but there was no one in the pond so far as he could see. Yet the voice persisted, "Over here! Here!"

The voice came from the fringe of flowers furthest from shore. "Take me! I am medicine" the voice said over and over.

Sky Watcher entered the water and waded out until he was neck deep and within arm's reach from the flower where the voice came from. "Take me and I will make your grandmother well."

Sky Watcher reached out, slipped his fingers under the cup of the flower.

"No! No! All of me," the flower screamed.

Sky Watcher took hold of the stalk with both hands and pulled with all his strength. The plant wouldn't give. As he had seen some elder people do, Sky Watcher had to dig up the plant from its bed, except that he had to do it underwater. He could stay underwater only for so long, only as long as his lungs could stand being without air. By the time that he had lifted the plant from its bed, Sky Watcher was gasping and buckling at the knees, near collapse.

One night some months later, Sky Watcher stood with his grandmother on their watching rock studying the stars and the star world. As they stood there, Sky Watcher told his grandmother once more how he had received his gift from the Star World, and how it had taken all his strength and endurance to retrieve it.

"Yes," his grandmother said. "That's the way with learning. If you want to know and understand something, you must learn what may seem unnecessary and demanding."

Years later, Sky Watcher could read the stars from the way they danced and they changed the colours of their garments.

CEDAR — For centuries now, people have looked on trees and forests from several different points of view. Many books referred to forests as wilderness wherein roamed wild and ferocious beasts. They were stands that occupied land that could be better used as farmland and, better still, as residential or industrial development, as pulp, timber and firewood. They were resources that brought profit and progress. Cut the trees down. Clear the forest. Make way for progress.

It is only in recent times that some scientists and citizens have come to realize that trees serve purposes other than as money-making materials. Trees lend beauty to the countryside. Trees and forests anchor the ground to keep the soil in place. Trees absorb water, keep the earth and the soil moist, and yield moisture to the atmosphere. Trees and forests are windbreakers. They shelter birds, animals and insects who sow the seeds that will grow as trees, and who perform services to the earth that benefit humans.

Modern men and women are at long last waking up to the fact that trees and forests are absolutely essential for humankind's well-being and survival. They are just beginning to grasp what our ancestors knew a long time ago.

It was a young man who, when asked by a manitou what he wanted, asked for medicine for good health for his people. His wish was granted only after his death. Strange green plants that later became evergreens began their growth and life on top of his grave.

Among the pine, spruce, balsam, tamarack, and ferns that sprang from the grave was the cedar. Few trees served as many purposes. Its branches, soft and aromatic, were used as matting in wigwaum. They were used as roofing for lean-tos. Its roots and resins were converted into thongs, binding, sealing, cement, lacing and ribbing for canoes. In winter, when there were no green vegetables available, cooks stuffed the inner pith of cedar into rabbits and partridges to give the meal vitamin C that men and women need for good health. It was for this practice that the Mohawks called our people Adirondacks, "Bark Eaters."

Long before Jacques Cartier chanced upon this continent, the

Anishinaubaek and other North American Indians were using cedar as medicine. In the first winter that Cartier and his crew spent here, they caught scurvy owing to the lack of vitamin C in their diet of salted fish and meat. The Indian healers knew the symptoms and cure for scurvy. Lucky thing for the newcomers; they might have all died out.

BIRCH — Our ancestors called it "weegwauss" for its apparent fragility and gleam; it was anything but fragile. There were great stands of birch: yellow birch, silver birch, white birch. It was one of Kitchi-Manitou's great gifts to the earth and all living beings.

"Take me," the birch tree said, "and I will make your travel upon this Path of Life a little less arduous."

The Anishinaubaek looked at the trees and asked themselves, "What can this tree do for us? How can this tree, with its delicate, brittle white tissue of bark, help?"

They didn't learn what the tree could do in one day. It was likely that it took many generations to learn the properties of the tree and its bark. Once they learned that it was water resistant, the Anishinaubaek used sheets of birch bark as roofing and siding for their lodgings. The sheets were light, durable, portable. When a family moved, it packed its building materials and used them in their new home.

As a wigwaum the birch kept the rain and the sleet from drenching people. Then someone or several figured that birch bark would serve as the most suitable material for a boat. It was light and durable, light enough for a man to carry the canoe overland from one body of water to another. Two paddlers could travel up to 80 miles on one day. When rain overtook the travellers, it was a simple matter for them to go ashore, turn their canoe upside down and "voila" it was a shelter.

In their travels the Anishinaubaek took very little with them; a bow and arrows, an axe, a blanket, a knife and, in their pouches, tobacco, a pipe, corn, a talisman, medicines, tinder, a tissue of birch bark, and flint.

What they needed along the way: dishes, baskets, containers, whatever, the travellers made from birch bark. Fire was easily made, even in winter. The traveller struck two flints together which contained the spirit of fire. The sparks of fire lit on the tinder, causing it to smoulder. To bring the spark and coal to flame, the firemaker touched the tissue of birch bark to the tiny coals and blew. A flame was born which, when fed with kindling, became a fire.

Birch bark is sacred, everything is sacred. It carries and gives life to fire which gives light and warmth. Birch bark is sacred in another way. Medicine people spoke to the manitous. When the manitous answered, the medicine people wrote down on birch bark what the manitous said. Besides the words of the manitous, the medicine people of the Medaewaewin wrote down their dreams, songs and events on birch bark scrolls. Birch bark is sacred, made so by the spiritual nature of the messages between humans and the manitous that dealt with the health of body, soul and spirit and the attainment of inner peace.

Today only a few people can read the scrolls. Most know next to nothing about them. To them, the birch can be turned into quill boxes to be sold as souvenirs, or cut down, good as firewood or lumber for flooring.

TOBACCO — Among the articles that men and women carried in their bundles was tobacco. When a hunter killed an animal, he offered tobacco to the victim's spirit out of respect and regret. It was also an act of thanksgiving to Kitchi-Manitou. When he passed through a dangerous place, the traveller offered tobacco. When Medicine people gathered medicine, they offered tobacco in thanksgiving.

Men and women kept in mind their debt to the earth, the plants, the elements, and the good will of the manitous. Tobacco smoke carried their thoughts and their feelings to the animals and to Kitchi-Manitou. And they smoked the pipe with each other as a sign of friendship.

How did the Anishinaubaek get tobacco? Some say that Nana'b'oozoo stole the tobacco from his own father, not knowing that the old man was his own father. Anyway, he got away with it. In another story, Nana'b'oozoo challenged his father to a fight. The father easily defeated his rash son. Instead of killing his son as he could have done, Ae-pungishimook, as he was called, offered Nana'b'oozoo a pipe and tobacco as sign of reconciliation. Nana'b'oozoo readily accepted.

At home, Nana'b'oozoo nearly caused a panic among his kin and neighbours the first time that he smoked the pipe. People ran from his shouting "A fire eating man! A bear-walker." Others caught Nana'b'oozoo and threw him into a lake to save him from burning up.

SWEET GRASS — Akeewaedin, a young man, came to the Land of Ice, Snow, and cold. Here he met Abi-boonikae, Wintermaker, who told him that the North was the home of the Bear with power to cure diseases. Abi-boonikae gave Akeewaedin a braid of sweet grass, the first plant to grow upon the bosom of Mother Earth. The incense of sweet grass in your home will keep evil away.

SAGE — Ningo-ipee-anung, another son, wandered all the way to the foothills of the mountains, loftier than any to be found in the land of the Anishinaubaek. Here roamed birds and animals unlike those to be seen in Anishinaubae-aki. The plants too were different. Ningo-ipee-anung worked his way through the Land of Mountains until he came to a great sea. As he stood gazing out over the waters as far as the horizon, an old man quietly drew up beside him. When Ningo-ipee-anung noticed that he had a companion, he asked the old man what lay beyond the horizon and whether there was land on the other side. The old man told Ningo-ipee-anung that he was the Watcher, there to keep wanderers from continuing their journey that leads only to the Land of Souls. They will all eventually get there in old age, but some slip by me while they are still young. To keep you in health, take this sage, "maewishkotae-wuhnshk." Put the sage to the sacred flames of fire and the fumes will cleanse you and keep you in health.

TREES AS SHELTER

When Mother Earth, disguised as an old woman whom they had nursed back to health, asked four friends what they were looking for far from home, one of the friends asked for good hunting and health. What brought the young man to make this request was the hardship that people suffered in winter when blizzards tore across meadows and lakes and through forests. Even birds and animals suffered, and did what they could to survive. Some birds went south. Some animals made dens for themselves to escape the storms. Many, such as deer, wolves, foxes, and wolverines, who couldn't go south or dig holes, did what they could to keep from freezing or starving to death. It was a reasonable, unselfish request.

The old woman gave the young man a bundle of powder. As she had instructed him, the young man made a beverage from the powder, which he then drank. Nothing happened. It was only after the young man died many years later that his wish was granted in a remarkable way.

From his burial mound there grew green plants that increased in size and height as trees. These trees multiplied and by and by became great forests. Just what the young man had wanted for his people. Cedars, pines, spruces, balsams, ferns were what people, birds and animals
needed as winter sheltering and feeding grounds.

Deer take shelter in cedar groves and woods in summer and winter, and there gave birth to their fawns. They also fed there. Partridges, snow birds, chickadees and other winter birds make cedar trees and forests their homes and feeding grounds. Rabbits huddle under the branches of cedars, balsam and spruces, out of reach of wolves and foxes. At night they frolic and picnic beneath the arms of these great trees.

A long time ago chickadees adopted cedars as their special homes.

When the little chickadees learned that they were to go south at the end of the summer, they were excited. They played tag with even greater energy in order to exercise and make their wings strong for the long flight south.

One little chickadee, too careless in play and in flight, flew into a tree and broke its wing. Gone were its dreams of going south to avoid the snows and the cold. Instead it faced its end.

The other birds came to bid farewell before leaving. And off they flew. But the broken winged chickadee's parents, brothers and sisters did not go with the great flocks of birds who left. They stayed by the side of the broken-winged chickadee who kept its wing tucked in close to its side. His brothers and sisters brought it seeds to eat as if it were still a helpless infant. It begged its parents to leave before it was too late, and to let him be.

But his family would not leave.

One morning before his family woke up, the little chickadee set out. It would walk south.

But before he had gone too far, his family overtook him. They pleaded with him to stay where he was and to rest his wing, but he would not. He didn't want to be responsible for the deaths of his family.

As the days passed, it grew colder. Clouds curtained the sun, and snow began to fall. Already evening shadows were falling.

"We must find shelter" they said, looking at a birch.

"Better you find shelter elsewhere," the birch rasped.

"My friend. Can you not allow us to stay under your root for the night?" the cripple's mother pleaded. "My son's lame and needs a rest. It's so very cold."

"I'm already looking after one of your kin. I cannot look after more than one. Try another place."

Downcast, the stragglers hobbled away.

By and by they trudged to a halt under the limbs of a huge oak.

"Let's camp here for the night. It's getting too dark" they said.

"The place is already spoken for" the Oak's deep voice rumbled. "There's no more room!"

"Just for one night," the mother chickadee pleaded. "We have a cripple."

"No matter. Make your shelter elsewhere."

On the stragglers plodded until they stood shivering under a tree whose thick lower limbs fairly drooped to the ground.

"My friends. What keeps you here? Why aren't you with the rest of your kin in the land of never-ending summer?"

The mother chickadee explained how her son's accident had prevented her family from making the journey south.

"My friends," the cedar said, "I have never turned away a wayfarer. You're welcome to stay as long as you want. Help yourselves to my seeds. I cannot promise to keep you warm, but I will shield you from the wind."

"You are more than kind," the mother chickadee answered.

The family found a small grotto under an overhanging bough that drooped to the ground. It was warmer than they thought was possible. And there was more than enough food.

Here in this evergreen forest of cedars, spruces, pines and balsams the family of chickadees remained. To keep warm, they flit from branch to branch, from tree to tree. All the while they called out to each other "N'sheemaehn! N'sheemaehn!" meaning either Brother! or Sister!

In the spring the migrants from the south returned. It was a joyful reunion that they all celebrated with a Pow Wow. Never again did the chickadees go south for the winter.

TREES AS FOUNTAINS

THE MAPLE — So much did the maple tree mean to the Anishinaubaek that they called it "inin-autik," the man tree. No other tree yields as much sap or as sweet a drink as does the maple. Come mid-March, give or take a few days either way, the Maple trees can no longer take in another drop of water or hold back what they've taken in during the past year. They must shed and change their life fluid as women change their blood once a month.

When the maples shed their life fluids, the Anishinaubae peoples referred to the overflow of sap as the flowing or the spilling. "Zeegwun," they said of it. And they used the same term to refer to the first or earliest period of spring. For them, spring began the day the maple trees brimmed over and dampened their sides.

It was a time for celebration, a festival. The flow of sap marked the beginning of a new season. Once again, as it has done for years and as it would do many more years still to come, the man tree would yield its life fluids, sweet to drink. And with the magic of fire, the sweet fluid would be changed into syrup and even into toffee and sugar. Soon after the blue-birds and the robins return and fill the woods with music. Hibernating animals awaken from their long winter's sleep. Within days, weeks, flowers and grasses return to life.

When the sap ran it was sugaring time. Families flocked to the sugar bush. Everybody made birch bark containers while children watched to learn how the adults did it. Then men and women notched the trees and inserted a wedge into the notch. They set a container under the homemade spile to catch the life fluid of the maple.

A central fireplace was set up. Wood gatherers delivered wood. Sap gatherers drew sap to be boiled down to syrup, and then into blocks of sugar. The sap was boiled in birch bark containers or in earthenware containers.

Contrary to some reports, the Anishinaubaek did not dunk rocks into boiling water to boil sap to syrup. They had more ingenuity than to amass a large pile of rocks, build a fire, pitch rocks into the sap, and then extract them with some instrument without leaving grit or ashes in the syrup. Just imagine dipping and lifting syrup covered rocks from syrup. Or take into account the time factor. Even with metal cauldrons sitting directly over coals and flames, it takes hours, and many pails of sap to reduce the sap to syrup form. Has anyone bothered to calculate how long it would take to obtain one gallon of syrup by dunking hot rocks in the sap?

Just how the Anishinaubaek learned that maple sap could be converted to syrup and sugar, no one can say. Experiment or accidental discovery? More likely accidental discovery, as the following story exemplifies.

A certain young woman, newly married, was fond of company. She didn't like being left alone. As soon as her new husband was gone in the morning, the young woman went to her neighbours' to join other women in tanning hides or sewing them into garments.

On this one day the young woman prepared a stew. Then she ran off to join her friends. With so many stories to listen to, she couldn't give as much attention to either her sewing or her stew. When she remembered her stew, the young woman ran home to tend to the meal that she was preparing for her husband. She was just in time. Not having enough water, she poured sap over her stew before running back to her companions.

Back and forth she raced between her fireplace and the community gathering place. Each time that she returned home she added more sap to her stew. Strange. Her stew was getting thicker and stickier by the hour. It was also smelling sweeter, like berries, blossoms.

While the young woman was scratching her head, mystified by the strange behaviour of her stew, her husband returned home with a deer.

"Mmmm!" he murmured. "What are you cooking? Smells good!"

He reached into the pot and fished out a piece of meat. His wife looked on nervously as he blew on the meat.

"Mmmm!" he sighed. Never had he tasted anything as good or as sweet. What a wonderful woman he had married.

And that, according to the Anishinaubae story-tellers, was how the Anishinaubaek discovered how to make syrup and sugar from the sap of maple trees.

No wonder the Anishinaubaek had such a high regard for the maple.

Plants and trees are marvelous creations. Neither animals nor humans can live without them. How else can they be regarded but in terms of wonder. Year after year they yield more than enough to feed every living, moving being: fruit, vegetables, nuts, drink of every different kind, apples, pears, peaches, cherries, billberries, grapes, walnuts, hazelnuts, acorns, maple sap, labrador tea, cedar tonic, potatoes, corn, wild rice.

It is remarkable that a tiny seed or a nut should anchor itself in a tiny crevice in a rock, sink its roots and thrust itself as a tree 80 to 120 feet into the air, and live up to 300 or 500 years.

A tree may bend and creak and even lose a few limbs under gales and twisters, crack and snap in sub-zero weather, and splinter under a thunderbolt, but it will not loosen its grip upon its bed.

When a tree dies it becomes part of the earth and adds to the mass of the earth.

The Anishinaubaek were well aware of their debt to plants and trees.

INSECTS, BUGS, LITTLE CREATURES

Once upon a time there lived a poor little girl in a city of concrete, steel, and glass; neon signs and lights flashed and skipped; planes,
trains, and cars poisoned the air with choking dark fumes; trucks, buses,
and radios roared and thundered on the floor of the concrete canyons. It
was a city of wealth and ambitious mayors.

In this city where people had loads of money and culture, and
could buy anything, this poor little girl had nothing to eat except potato
chips and pizza, and nothing to drink but Kool-Aid. Her only toys were a
TV and a VCR, a stereo, a cell phone and a computer. Of her few toys this
poor little girl's favourite was her TV which she turned on as soon as she
woke up in the morning and turned off only at the last minute before
boarding a bus to take her to school. The first thing that this poor little
girl did on her return home from school was to run upstairs to her room

and turn on her beloved TV.

It told this poor little girl many things that she didn't know. She didn't have to pester her TV with questions, and it didn't growl or snap at her to "keep quiet."

Of all the programs that her beloved TV served her, this poor little girl liked none better than the vacation ads that invited families to spend their holidays in Muskoka or in the Kawarthas. Every morning and evenings loons yodeled, accompanied by an orchestra. Tame deer ate pretzels right off children's hands. In the background an orchestra played. Birds warbled in the trees and the sun shone from morning till night. Somewhere in the back a drummer bashed a tin can. Families smiled and laughed as they stuffed themselves with barbecued hamburgers, hot dogs and steaks. Young people sang as they loitered around a case of beer. Children frolicked in a concrete swimming pool.

So much did this poor little girl like what she saw on TV that she begged her parents to take her on a vacation. "Too expensive" they told her. She cried, she whimpered. And so, to comfort their daughter, the parents took their poor little girl to the best and worst malls and plazas in the city of splendour.

These week-end tours of malls and plazas did little to make this poor little girl feel better. "Someday" she told herself, "I'm going to go to Muskoka to listen to real loons and feed real deer."

To fulfill her dream of spending a vacation in Muskoka, the poor little girl would have to have a load of money. And the best way of amassing a pile of money was by going to university and working hard. This the little girl did.

By the time that she graduated from university with a degree, the little girl had saved a tidy sum of money by working in fast food outlets every week-end in malls, enough to pay for a holiday in Honey Harbour. At last, after 12 years of drudgery in school and at work, the poor girl was about to make her dream come true.

She and her girl friends rented a cottage for two weeks. To make sure that the vacation of her dreams would be just like the ones that a she saw on TV, the young woman and her friends took a portable radio, a CD player, a portable TV, cellular phones, lap-tops, frozen TV dinners, hamburgers, hot dogs, steaks and several cases of beer.

"Ah! This is the life!" the girls gushed as they hoisted beer to their lips and swiveled their hips to the clang and bang of heavy metal sound. Hamburgers and hot dogs sizzled and smoked.

But what's this?

Even before the girls got comfortable, mosquitoes, black flies, sand flies, deer flies, horse flies, nits, gnats and their kin attacked. The girls squirmed and twisted, slapped and scratched their arms, legs and faces. But they couldn't beat off the insects.

To escape, the girls retreated into the cottage. A swarm of mosquitoes followed them inside. Desperate, the girls turned off the lights. The mosquitoes and black flies found them.

When morning came, the girls packed their vacation supplies and fled back to the city.

The poor young woman who had dreamed of a holiday in Ontario's vacation land wrote of her ordeal in the Mope and Wail. From then on, she declared, she would spend her week-ends and vacations in the best malls, admiring the latest displays, the newest fashions, and eating formulated fast foods.

This young woman is just one of millions of people who believe that insects have no reason for their existence and should be exterminated. When people began to find insects offensive and wished for their destruction, they made poisons, called herbicides, to kill them off.

But the Anishinaubae peoples and other North American Indians believed that, though insects were nuisances at times, they were bothersome only for short periods. They were created for a purpose. Our ancestors may have known more about insects than they are given credit for today. And they told what they knew through stories.

BEES — Every spring the blanket of snow that covers Mother Earth melts away. Grasses and flowers spring to life: violets, little white flowers, leeks, trilliums. And before the trilliums fade and die after three weeks of life, lilac and apple and cherry blossoms decorate the trees and scent the air.

Bees are everywhere, as if called and brought into being by some invisible force. There are bees beyond counting, as many as stars in the sky, buzzing around apple and cherry trees, tending to the blossoms. They are hungry, starved for nectar. As they go from blossom to blossom sipping life-giving nectar, they pick up pollen and carry it to the next blossom, and to as many blossoms as they will visit. They will fertilize the blossoms that will then turn into apples, pears, peaches and nuts.

In taking care of the needs of Mother Earth and plants, bees look after their own needs, present and future. The nectar that the bees take back to their hive is turned into honey by honey making bees. Already in early spring bees are storing away food for the coming winter.

Until the bees and their kin pollinate blossoms, no fruit or vegetables grow. Birds and animals have little to eat. Bears depend upon bees to complete their work before they can have enough to eat.

Bears have a sweet tooth; they were born with a sweet tooth. They eat strawberries, blackberries, raspberries by the handsful and when there's nothing else, ants, roots and bark.

A long time ago a certain bear accidentally found that honey was sweet and good to eat. Immediately after his meal the bear told his kin about the goodness of honey. In no time the bears were doing little else but raiding bees' hives wherever the bees set their hives, in hollow logs, under brush piles, or high up, suspended from the limb of a tree.

All that the bees could do was to buzz around bear's head and threaten while the bear ate his fill. Start over was what the bees did after the freeloading bear left.

Before long the bees wearied of making honey for bears. It was as if they were working for bears and not for themselves. At the rate that the bears were helping themselves to the honey, it looked as if the bees wouldn't have enough food to keep them alive till the next spring.

Even the manitous were helping themselves to the food that the bees were making for themselves. One of the worst thieves was Nana'b'oozoo who, if he could get a meal without working, would simply help himself to someone's meal.

While Nana'b'oozoo was scooping honey from a hive and licking his fingers, the bees did the only thing they could do, dress him down and call him a thief. It would serve him right if fruit and vegetables didn't grow, and the birds and the animals were to grow and go away from the land.

"How so?" Nana'b'oozoo asked.

The bees explained.

Nana'b'oozoo was alarmed. No bees! No apples, peaches, pears; just roots! bark! moss! Hunger. How could such a thing be prevented? How could bees be helped? They were very small. Nana'b'oozoo could do no better than arm each bee with a little barb that he pulled off from rose bushes.

The bees didn't think too much of the little barbs affixed to the ends of their noses. How could they frighten or drive anyone off with such flimsy weapons if their little stingers could be regarded as weapons? But when they drove off the first bear, crying and squealing and crashing through the woods, the bees were proud of their stingers. All the birds and the animals came to respect bees.

Since that day a long time ago, animals and birds have pretty much left bees to do what no other creatures can do, help trees bring forth their fruit and plants their vegetables.

FIREFLIES — LIGHTNING BUGS — High up in the tallest mountains and in the most distant clouds live thunderbirds and their children, kin of eagles that live on earth. Only a few people have ever seen them, and those who set eyes on them say that thunderbirds are as big as polar bears. When they blink, lightning shoots from their eyes, and when they beat their wings, thunder rumbles and crashes across the sky.

Most of the time these large birds go about quietly doing their work, looking after Mother Earth, seeing to it that she is clean and her thirst cared for. It's as if the sky is empty and uninhabited. But when the thunderbirds notice that Mother Earth needs to be refreshed, they perform a ceremony. They play ball to create lightning, thunder, wind and rain. Then they rest.

Little thunderbirds watch their parents play. They are no different from other children who like to play. Play was all they wanted to do.

Those little thunderbirds ran; they raced, they jumped, they danced, they rolled on the clouds, they threw raindrops at each other, they ate snowflakes, they chewed icicles, they tore chunks of clouds, they pulled each other's feathers, and they climbed up one side of the rainbow and slid down the other side.

While they played, the little thunderbirds laughed and shouted, they sang and chattered.

While their little thunderbirds played and had fun, the mothers worried. They expected their little ones to get hurt at any moment. Many times they had to shout to remind their little thunderbirds to be careful, but that didn't do much good for long. The little thunderbirds promised to be careful, but soon after forgot and were playing as hard as before. The mothers scolded their little thunderbirds and punished them by making them sit on a hard cloud, but that didn't do much good either.

It got so bad one day that the mother thunderbirds had to sit on their little ones to keep them quiet. But their little ones didn't stay still. They moved, they turned, they rolled over, they tossed, they twisted, and they asked for drinks of rain water. They just would not keep quiet. With all the disturbance under them, the mothers didn't get any rest.

Finally one mother couldn't put up with any more nonsense. She said to the other mothers, "Let them play ball."

At first some mother thunderbirds didn't want their little ones to play ball. They were afraid that their little ones might get hurt. But most of the mother thunderbirds were in favour of letting the little thunderbirds play ball. They would watch and make sure that the little ones didn't get hurt.

When the little thunderbirds heard that their mothers were going to let them play ball, they were excited.

But before they started, their mothers made them promise to be careful. They were not to go near the edge of the clouds. They were to take care that they didn't hurt one another. And they were not to let the ball drop through the holes in the clouds.

The little thunderbirds promised to be careful.

One of the mommies brought out a shiny yellow ball and threw it out to the little thunderbirds.

The little thunderbirds started to play at once. They kicked the ball and chased it, they hit it with their wings and ran after it. They caught it and threw it. Each time they kicked the ball, each time they hit the ball, and each time it bounced, the skies rumbled. THUMP! THUMP! THUMP! THUMP! The little thunderbirds played just like big thunderbirds, and they made thunder. And when they laughed, their eyes sparkled and flashed lightning. Thunder and lightning; thunder and lightning.

But alas! Just when they were having the most fun, a little thunder-bird dropped the big shiny yellow ball. Before he could pick it up, it fell through a hole in the clouds and it fell down to the earth. There it burst with a mighty CRASH. There was a huge sunburst and shower of sparks.

That was the end of the game and the end of the big shiny yellow ball. But the sparks didn't go out. On summer nights these little sparks fly around. These little sparks became fireflies or lightning bugs.

The little thunderbird who dropped the ball was heartbroken. Indeed, all the little thunderbirds were near tears for having lost the ball. But their mothers weren't angry. They didn't say anything at all.

It made no difference. It didn't cheer up the little thunderbirds. All they wanted was their ball. All they wanted to do was to play ball. They didn't want to do anything else. They were as unhappy as could be.

All day they walked about as if they would never smile again. And they might not have ever smiled again if the little thunderbird who dropped the ball had not come up with an idea.

Her idea was for all of them to ask their mothers to let them go down to earth and to look for their ball. If it was broken, they would bring back the pieces and their mothers could mend the ball.

It was such a good idea that the little thunderbirds cheered up. They didn't wait. They ran to their mothers asking "Mommy! Can we do down to earth to look for our ball? Please, mommy! Please, please, please. We'll come right back."

But the mother thunderbirds didn't like the idea. They were afraid that their little thunderbirds might lose their way, or hurt themselves, or get too tired to come back. And they thought that it was too dangerous for little thunderbirds to go to the land of human beings. The mother thunderbirds said "No! You may not go."

The little thunderbirds cried and cried. They complained "You never let us do anything. You never let us go anywhere. We always have to stay here." And they cried louder. They cried as if they would never stop.

Finally the mother thunderbirds felt sorry for their little ones. Besides, they wanted some quiet in the skies. They decided to let their little thunderbirds go. They said, "You may go down to earth to look for your ball. But you must promise to be careful. You may go down only after the sun goes down and you must come home before sun-up. And you must be quiet, quiet as stars, or else you'll wake up human beings and monsters. Do you understand? Promise?"

The little thunderbirds promised to be careful and to do what their mothers wanted them to do.

They dried their tears and smiled and laughed, so happy were they.

The little thunderbirds wanted to leave at once, but of course they couldn't because the sun was still up. They waited and watched the sun, but the sun took its time as if it didn't want to lie down and go to sleep. The little thunderbirds were put out with the sun for staying up. They wished that the sun would hurry and go to sleep.

But at last the sun lay down behind some mountains and put out his light.

The moment that the little thunderbirds had been waiting for had come. "Can we go now? Can we go now?" they cried out.

"Just a moment! Wait!" the mother thunderbirds said. "You must put on your moccasins before you go because you must not walk on the ground in your bare feet."

The little thunderbirds put their moccasins on and they fluttered down to earth. They made not a sound.

Even before they landed on the ground, the little thunderbirds saw flying sparks floating around near the ground. They knew that these little sparks were pieces from their shiny ball. And they hurried to catch all the sparks as quickly as they could. They ran here and there in the dark wherever the sparks flashed.

At first the little thunderbirds were careful not to make a sound. But before long they were having so much fun, they forgot. They started to laugh and to race to see who would catch the most sparks. Besides, it was dark; they couldn't see. They ran into trees and stubbed their toes. Of course they cried out when they got hurt.

"QUIET! GO HOME!" a voice boomed out like thunder in the dark. Right afterwards there was another voice, "Pipe down or else I'm coming out with a stick."

The little thunderbirds were so startled by the booming voice and the word "stick" that they dropped their sparks and beat it out of there as fast as they could go.

When they got home the little thunderbirds went straight to their beds and fell asleep at once.

In the morning, after breakfast, the mother thunderbirds asked their little ones where their moccasins were. But the little thunderbirds didn't know. They looked around their nests and, not finding their moccasins, asked their mothers to find them.

That night the mother thunderbirds sent their little ones to earth to find their moccasins and to bring them back.

As soon as the sun went to bed the little thunderbirds went down to earth to find their moccasins.

It was a good thing that the moon was shining or else the little thunderbirds would not have been able to see. They found their moccasins, but just as they were about to pick them up, voices shouted at them from every part of the forest. "They're my shoes! They're my shoes! They're my shoes! Don't you touch! Don't you touch!"

The little thunderbirds thought that human beings, or even monsters, were shouting. They were so frightened that they shot into the air and flew home without their moccasins. They were so frightened that they didn't want to go to earth again. "They can have our moccasins" they said.

Next night the little thunderbirds' mothers came down to earth to look for the lost moccasins.

As they looked around in the forest voices screamed at them. "They're my shoes! They're my shoes! Leave them alone! Don't you touch!"

The mother thunderbirds felt sorry for these night birds who were shrieking in the forest. They decided to let the earthbirds have the moccasins. They would make new ones for their little thunderbirds.

When you go into the forest on a spring day you may see these little yellow slippers that human beings called Lady's Slippers or Lady's Moccasins. These were the little moccasins that the little thunderbirds left behind. And when the sun goes down at night and just before it comes up in the morning you will hear the earthbirds that human beings know as whippoorwills call out, "They're my shoes! They're my shoes! Don't you touch! Don't you touch!" They are the moccasins that the little thunderbirds wore and lost when they came down to earth to look for their ball that had broken into zillions of pieces and came to life as fireflies.

CICADAS — THE PAINTERS — Every day in every home in every village there takes place a battle between children and their parents over food. It's a battle that's been going on since the beginning of time.

"Eat your carrots!"

"No, I don't like them."

"But they're good for you; make you big and strong."
"I don't want to be and strong."
"It's better than getting sick."
"I want honey and maple syrup."

If the struggle wasn't over carrots, it was over some other vegetable or fruit.

And children did have a point, not a big point perhaps but a point nevertheless. In those old days all vegetables, fruits, flowers and leaves were green, and without flavour. To give their food flavour, people poured honey and maple syrup on everything.

It is not a good thing for people to quarrel either before or during a meal. A meal is a life and health saving act, meant to be a pleasant celebration.

But what were parents to do to avoid these daily clashes with their children?

It became such a big issue that chiefs and elders met to discuss how they might make children eat their food without whining and acting up. For all their wisdom, the elders couldn't think of anything worthwhile.

They needed someone with greater inventiveness than they possessed, someone like Nana'b'oozoo. Him the elders invited to resolve the difficulty. They asked him to find a way of making food more attractive and tasty, and meals more pleasant.

Even for a manitou such as Nana'b'oozoo to make food more appealing was daunting. It required all the powers that he possessed.

When Nana'b'oozoo decided to paint the fruits and vegetables, and to give each fruit and vegetable a flavour, he didn't know whether parents and their children would like the coloured, flavoured food any better than the old foods. It was worth a try.

It meant a lot of hard work. First there were many tubs to make, paints to mix, and last there were billions of fruits and vegetables to paint.

All he needed after he'd made tubs and mixed paints was a

brush. At Nana'b'oozoo's feet grew a small plant whose ends resembled bristles. This he used as a paintbrush.

Nana'b'oozoo vanished the moment he set to work. The only sign that Nana'b'oozoo was at work was a rush of wind, the rustle of leaves, the bending of rushes by the river side.

The next morning, the children who had got up earlier than others, clapped their hands and cried in delight.

"Look! Come and see! Someone's painted the apples and everything," and the children ran to trees and to the meadows.

"They smell so good!" they exclaimed as they reached for and plucked fruit and vegetables and put them to their mouths.

The children spoke no words to express their delight in the flavour of the fruit and vegetables except to smack their lips and to hum "mmmmm."

At the end of the day the people all agreed that Nana'b'oozoo had done what nobody else could have done.

The next morning the first child to get up ran outside to be the first to taste the new kind of food.

"Waaah!" the child wailed. "Someone's smeared everything with something. Now we can't eat anything!"

Everybody rushed outdoors. The child wasn't lying. Everything was covered with a thin film of white powder. Someone had ruined Nana'b'oozoo's work.

They rushed to Nana'b'oozoo's lodge. Half choked, they jabbered out their story.

"Who did this?" Nana'b'oozoo asked.

"We don't know," the people answered. "Do something! Save our fruit and vegetables!"

"That I'll do first, then I'll hunt down the person who did this," Nana'b'oozoo gave his word without thinking. The same moment he was gone. By nightfall all the fruits and vegetables were once more redecorated. His work was done and he himself was done in. Nana'b'oozoo went to bed without eating.

But the someone had come along during the night and sprinkled white powder on everything. Once more Nana'b'oozoo had to get up and to work until dark. Only his love for children kept him going.

Soon after he started repainting, Nana'b'oozoo heard sharp, derisive laughter. For the first few times that the cutting laughter pealed across the treetops, Nana'b'oozoo let the laughter pass as a bird call, nothing to pay attention to. But after a while the laughter, cutting like that of a kingfisher, began to grate upon his nerves. By and by Nana'b'oozoo recognized the voice as that of his brother Pukawiss.

Nana'b'oozoo's temper shot up at once like fireworks. His brother was making him work, redo everything, and laughing at him. If Nana'b'oozoo could have throttled his brother then he would have done so, but he could not very well leave his work less than half finished. He could only threaten to wring Pukawiss's neck. Pukawiss laughed all the louder.

The teasing went on.

Days later a large fly, 3-4 times larger than the common fly, lit on an apple tree that Nana'b'oozoo was decorating. Nana'b'oozoo had seen these flies before, but had paid little attention to them. He didn't know where they came from or what they did.

The big fly annoyed him, sitting there doing nothing while he, Nana'b'oozoo, was unable to rest or to eat a proper meal during the day.

"Don't you do anything?" Nana'b'oozoo demanded gruffly.

"No. Why?" the overgrown fly asked.

"Would you mind spelling me off for a little bit while I go check with the chief to see how much more he wants me to do."

"Be glad to," the overgrown fly answered. "Just tell me what you want done."

"Paint all the vegetables, fruits and berries. I won't be gone too long. Then you can go back to what you were doing. . . . Just one other thing; don't you stop work!"

"I won't!" the big fly assured Nana'b'oozoo.

Nana'b'oozoo shot off like a shaft in chase of Pukawiss. Over hills, meadows, through forests, across the surface of lakes he flew. There were times when Nana'b'oozoo was at Pukawiss's heels and was about to reach out to nab him, but his brother spurted away in a rush, leaving Nana'b'oozoo far behind, panting and raging.

Not once did Nana'b'oozoo ever go back, so far as is known, to resume his work painting vegetables, fruits and nuts. He need not have worried. These big flies, whom the Anishinaubaek call Tissauwaesheehnk, The Painters, had their minds set on one thing only, to please Nana'b'oozoo and human beings. They didn't give Nana'b'oozoo another thought. Using their wings as brushes, the cicadas painted everything, leaves included. They still paint to this day, and ever since cicadas began to paint and give flavour to all the fruit and vegetables, children and their parents have battled less often than before over food.

BUTTERFLIES — It could be said that children invented butterflies. They didn't actually invent them, but they did inspire Nana'b'oozoo to bring them into being.

Away back in the beginning of the world, children had nothing to play with. Their eyes were dull with unhappiness, their arms and legs weak from moping about.

To see children go about as gloomy as old buzzards worried Nana'b'oozoo. As he saw it, children should laugh and clap their hands in glee, run and jump. Their eyes should sparkle in delight.

To find a way to make children happy Nana'b'oozoo went off by himself to a high mountain. There he asked the manitous to help him invent a game or create something that would bring children out of the doldrums. But for all his praying and thinking, Nana'b'oozoo could not come up with a single worthwhile idea that would brighten children's lives.

At the foot of the mountain Nana'b'oozoo picked up some pretty pebbles which he rolled around in his hands. He then pitched them behind him. Before they fell to the ground the pebbles turned into flying creatures. But Nana'b'oozoo didn't see them.

When children saw these little creatures for the first time, they opened their eyes wide in delight and ran after them. They called them Maemaegawauhnssiwuk, "little feathers that danced in the wind."

Butterflies opened children's eyes and uplifted their spirits. They were pretty, wearing pretty clothing while dancing from flower to flower. And they were out of the ordinary. They came into life and being as butterflies in stages. As butterflies they were in their fourth stage of existence and form. Before they were butterflies, they were in the chrysalis stage. Prior to that stage they were caterpillars. Girls didn't like them because they were creepy and homely. Their kin, tent caterpillars, gave all caterpillars a bad name by coming together once every few years and mulching all the leaves of trees in a forest. But they did this to help out the saplings and flowers on forest floor get some sunlight for their growth. Before caterpillars saw the light of day, they were some other creature in a cocoon. Butterflies were remarkable little creatures that reflected a remarkable aspect of life.

The old story of brightly coloured pebbles turning into butterflies is not too far off the natural evolution of a butterfly from the pebble-like form of a chrysalis.

Some of the things that butterflies do are reflected in the following story about the monarch butterfly and its association with the milkweed.

When butterflies came into the world and followed Nana'b'oozoo like a cloud of smoke to our land, adults and children were delighted as never before. Children ran after and caught these little creatures and carried them about in their hands. They showed their parents the new pets. They let them go only to catch them again. But some boys and girls were too rough. They closed their hands over their pets much too tightly. They bruised them. They bent their wings. They scraped the powdery colour off the wings of their pets, and even warped their antennae.

Parents and grandparents had often to remind the children, "Be careful! Don't hurt your friends! They aren't hurting you!" The children promised to be more careful, but some soon forgot and bruised their friends again. But the kinder children asked, "Who would hurt such beautiful creatures?" and they caressed their little friends and patted them, for they were as soft and light as feathers.

As the days grew shorter and cooler, the birds stopped chirping and they began to gather in flocks. Men and women put food away, and the grandmothers made warm clothing. "Winter can't be far behind," the elders said. "The birds are getting ready to go south. Soon many animals and insects will burrow into the ground or hide in some den or cave to escape the cold. Other animals will grow thick coats to help them survive the winter."

"And what will our pets do? Where will they go?" the children asked in alarm.

But no one knew, not even the elders who are supposed to know. "Wait and see! Kitchi-Manitou will let them know what to do" they explained.

And that is what happened. Kitchi-Manitou told the Brown Butterflies (Monarchs) to follow the birds and go south, as far south as their wings could carry them. All the rest went into hiding. Where they went, no one knew.

In the spring, after the snow melted, the butterflies reappeared as if by magic. There were thousands of them: blue, red, green, yellow, pink, purple, brown, white, every colour of the rainbow. There were striped, spotted, speckled, and two-toned butterflies dancing and weaving and floating and fluttering in the wind. They wafted from flower to flower. In honour of their coming and grace, women and girls made costumes and danced the "Flight of the Little Feathers."

But, of course, men and women and children weren't the only ones to regard the butterflies as beautiful. Birds took notice of the butterflies. So beautiful! So tempting! They looked good enough to eat. They were much prettier than worms or bugs or grubs.

Once the sparrows, robins, warblers, catbirds, kingbirds, and thrushes ate the butterflies and found that they tasted as good as they looked, the birds would eat nothing else but butterflies. And they were much easier to catch; nothing to it.

The butterflies were frightened. They were much too slow to escape the hungry birds. They were too weak to fight back. The birds plucked them out of the air or snatched them from blossoms. Not even their friends, the boys and girls, could keep the birds away.

The butterflies were afraid to venture out even to eat. They never knew when the end would come.

One little green butterfly saw a dark flash above, and heard the beat of wings. She darted under the leaf of a milkweed plant. She trembled and wheezed in fright.

"Why so frightened?" a voice asked.

The butterfly shrieked in terror. It screamed and trembled. It nearly slipped and fell to the ground below.

"I'm sorry! I didn't mean to frighten you," the voice said.

"W-w-w-w-w- who are y-y-y-y- you?" the little butterfly stammered.

"I'm the manitou of the milkweed," the voice said, and then asked again, "Why so frightened?"

"A bird is after me!" the butterfly gasped. "The birds are eating all of us alive. They're going to kill all of us. We can't sleep. We can't eat. We can't rest, ever. We're always afraid. I'm so tired of watching, hiding! Always wondering when I'm going to be set on and killed."

"Take the nectar from my blossoms. Eat, drink! My nectar is food, sap, and medicine, and the birds will bother you no more."

The butterfly wanted to believe. But he couldn't believe that the manitou's words could be true.

But there was nothing else, no other hope. The butterfly crept out from its hiding place under the leaf and crawled atop the milkweed blossom and sipped the nectar, and so good was the sap that the butterfly quite forgot the birds. Only when a crow closed its beak around it did the butterfly scream in terror. But instead of snapping its jaws shut, the crow coughed and spat out the butterfly.

The crow flew off, spitting and coughing and clearing its throat and sputtering "Yuk! Phew! Yuk! It tastes like rotten fish! Yagghh!" The crow flew off, screaming with all his might. "Yuk! Butterflies are yucky! Poison! Don't eat them!"

A few foolish birds tried to eat butterflies after that. But they too threw up. Butterflies were foul, no good to eat.

After that the birds left butterflies alone. They didn't eat them again. Yes, milkweed medicine was good. Ever since that time, monarch butterflies have taken most of their food from milkweed.

MOSQUITOES — If it weren't for mosquitoes and their brothers such as blackflies, humans would go on vacations and about their work without worrying about bites and stings and rashes. But mosquitoes and their kin are the bane of North American humans who want nothing but comfort and tans. They come at people in sorties and in swarms.

They assault men and women at work.

They harass old people and infants in their beds.

From dawn to dawn they draw drops of human blood.

Kill 500 and another 500 reserves replace their fallen comrades.

Nothing save smoke and cold can drive them off.

Crying Dog, a Cree from James Bay, refused to live in peace with his irksome neighbours.

"You're home early! Got a moose already?" his wife asked when Crying Dog returned home one day sooner than expected.

"I can't stand it anymore," he grumbled. "BLACKFLIES! MOSQUI-TOES! They're driving me insane!"

"My poor Honey Pot!" Mrs. Dog crooned.

Crying Dog blustered into their wigwaum where he settled on a bed of tamarack, going out of doors only to go to the washroom. He spent his days and nights wracking his brain, about what, Crying Dog refused to say.

While Crying Dog moped in his wigwaum, his wife did all the work that he should have been doing to put food in their bowls.

Only after the mosquitoes, blackflies and their kind had disappeared from the land did Crying Dog come out of his hiding place.

At last he was able to work in peace, and work he did to make up to his wife for what he made her do during his idleness. Feeling guilty, Crying Dog did extra work for his wife, children and his neighbours.

The mosquitoes and blackflies were gone, but they would be back in the spring. With this in mind, Crying Dog worked even harder during the winter months to put away enough food so that he wouldn't have to face mosquitoes and blackflies again when summer came.

It was while he and several of his Cree hunting friends were closing in on a moose that their method of ganging up on an animal gave Crying Dog the idea that they too ought to gang up on mosquitoes and blackflies and kill them all. He didn't say anything about his idea to his companions.

As soon as Crying Dog and his fellow hunters returned to their village, he went to the chief with his idea.

The chief's eyes narrowed. His mind opened. He'd be famous. His people would be known throughout the Land of the Great Turtle if he were to adopt Crying Dog's idea.

Crying Dog asked the chief to send a courier to all the Indian nations inviting their chiefs, headmen and warriors to come to a grand council, to be followed by the greatest battle ever waged on the face of Mother Earth.

The chief's couriers ran to every part of the Land of the Great Turtle inviting warriors of all nations to come to James Bay. Every warrior and chief promised to come, excited by the prospect of a free meal and additional honours by bashing a few heads.

Meanwhile, Crying Dog was busy filling the food racks with meat and fish to feed the immense number of warriors expected to arrive.

Came the day of days, sun washed and warm. As far as the eye could see, ear hear, sat chiefs, headmen and warriors upon the muskeg, sharpening their arrows, bending their bows in test, flexing their muscles in preparation for the war-path. Nothing mattered except the coups that would be counted; nothing more important than the eagle feathers that would be added to headdresses.

When the Cree chief and Crying Dog mounted a knoll to address the assembly, the warriors bent forward silently to hear the words of welcome and to learn the nature of the offence that they were to avenge, the identity of the enemy, his strength, his stronghold.

After the words of greeting and welcome uttered by the chief, Crying Dog stood up. He held up his hand for silence. There was not a sound, except for the buzzing of the flies.

"Brothers! Welcome. We are glad that you have come. You have come in brotherhood. And so long as you are here you are welcome to our mats, our fires, our bowls. Nobody's as good as the Cree in making you feel at home.

With the permission of my chief I have called you here to take up the war-club and to destroy once and for all time our greatest enemy. Simple defeat will not be enough. Nothing less than utter destruction will do. That's the way the White people do it. The enemy must be destroyed. Only then will they stop murdering our children in their cradle-boards; only then will he stop ravaging our elders in their sleep. The enemy must be wiped out.

"Ho! Ho! Ho!" the Dakotas and the Blackfeet chanted. "What are we waiting for? Cruel! Cruel!"

"We must carry the war-club to him," Crying Dog shouted. "We must search him out in the marshes, in the meadows, in the forests, in the trees, on the ground, over the waters, in the air. Nay! Wherever he may be found." Crying Dog did not finish, drowned out.

"Ho! Ho! Ho! Let us kill the cowards! Cut the speeches! The war-dance! They deserve to die! Who is the enemy, Crying Dog?" the voices demanded. "Yes, who is the enemy? Tell us!"

Crying Dog held up his hand. "They are here, in your midst, all around you," he shouted.

"Who? Who? Who?" the shouts grew louder, angrier.

"Mosquitoes, blackflies, sandflies, horseflies, mooseflies, deerflies, lice, ticks, nits and gnats," Crying Dog yelled, violently striking the air above him. The interpreter interpreted.

There was a moment of unearthly silence before the visiting chiefs, headmen and warriors grasped the meaning of Crying Dog's words. Thousands of voices thundered out over the muskeg and James Bay, "Kill Crying Dog;" "He's made fun of us;" "Tear him to pieces;" "We came all the way here to kill mosquitoes;" "Burn him." The crowd surged forward to seize Crying Dog, but in the ensuing confusion he escaped.

Midst threats, waving arms, unable to find Crying Dog, the warriors left.

Only after he was certain that all the warriors had gone did Crying Dog come out of hiding to return to his village and to his wig-waum. He set to work at once, despite the taunts of his neighbours, gathering roots and bark of tamarack, spruce, pine and cedar, fashioning bags and baskets, hundreds and thousands.

Then, with a bag slung over his shoulder or a basket under an arm, Crying Dog set out catching flies, picking them out of the air in flight or plucking them from leaves and grasses as they rested. He even snatched them from their nesting places in the water and under logs, wherever he could find them. As soon as a bag was full, Crying Dog would set it aside, bind it, and take another. From morning to night Crying Dog worked every day until all the bags were full and until there was not a mosquito or blackfly to be seen or heard anywhere.

It was already autumn, cool and chilly, when Crying Dog began to construct longhouses; so many did he put up that he made a town larger than any village ever seen in the north.

Crying Dog was tireless; as soon as he had hung the last door, he stored the bags of mosquitoes and blackflies in the longhouse warehouses. All that could be heard near the longhouses were the buzz and hum of mosquitoes and blackflies. Once in a while Crying Dog would stop to listen. To him it was nothing short of music. Still, he was not through.

Without resting, he started collecting firewood from driftwood, stumps, dead trees, and bushes until he had amassed a huge pile. When he had gathered enough wood, Crying Dog kindled a fire in each l onghouse to keep his captives comfortable and warm. Back and forth from one longhouse to the next Crying Dog walked to keep the fires burning every day. No matter how busy he was or how inclement the weather, Crying Dog could be heard singing.

On the coldest day in February, Crying Dog rose early. Entering the first longhouse he withdrew a large sack of buzzing insects which he cheerfully bore to the middle of the bay. He opened the bag. Mosquitoes, blackflies, sandflies and assorted other flies poured out of the bag at once, their humming strong and vibrant. They gained altitude, forming a black cloud above Crying Dog's head where they hovered a few minutes before they fell to the ice, clunk, clunk, clunk, frozen, dead ... stiff. Crying Dog stamped on some, at the same time saying, "That'll fix you. You'll never bother me again!" It took a good ten days to empty the bags. At the end of that time all that remained was an enormous black mountain of dead flies on the ice in the middle of the bay.

Spring came, as did ducks and geese and robins and sparrows, but no flies. There was not a single mosquito or blackfly to harass men or women or children. For the first time Crying Dog knew peace.

In mid-summer Crying Dog, hot from cutting wood for his wife, who had forgiven him, refreshed himself with a swim in the bay. Afterward, naked, he lay on the flat rocks to sun himself. While Crying Dog lay there, his eyes closed, he heard the hum of a mosquito. Even though he refused to believe it, Crying Dog could not mistake that hum, all too familiar. He sat up, looked around. To be sure, there was a mosquito flying around just above his head, out of reach. Crying Dog snapped off a willow branch with which he furiously beat the air to batter the mosquito, who quickly swerved beyond reach. Soon another mosquito arrived, enraging Crying Dog all the more. Then another and another. In a little while there was a swarm forming a small cloud whose humming and buzzing rang in Crying Dog's ears.

Then the mosquitoes attacked the naked Crying Dog, nipping his ears, his neck, his legs, his rump, his arms. Unable to beat off the mosquitoes, Crying Dog threw his branch away and plunged into the water. But as soon as he came up for air, the mosquitoes attacked again, forcing Crying Dog to submerge once more. Each time that the man came up gasping for air, the mosquitoes renewed their assault. In no time Crying Dog, exhausted and weak, floated to the surface as one drowned, except that he was still alive, barely.

It was said that the mosquitoes, assisted by blackflies, sandflies, horseflies, mooseflies, deerflies, lice, ticks, nits and gnats lifted Crying Dog out of the water and bore him through the air to a distant place somewhere in the remote north. There, after making a huge bag, the mosquitoes and their allies stuffed Crying Dog into it; inside, the man yelled and cried out, threatened vengeance, demanded release, all the while tearing at and clawing the sides of the bag in order to break out. The mosquitoes then made a lodge around the bag. In the autumn they gathered wood with which they kept the lodge warm and comfortable. On the coldest day of the winter the mosquitoes removed the bag containing Crying Dog and, bearing it high over the clouds, returned to the bay where the previous winter Crying Dog had released the mosquitoes to freeze. Above the clouds and directly over the bay the mosquitoes dumped Crying Dog out of the bag. His body was found by his fellow tribesmen.

Afterwards people said, "Don't let little things bug you."

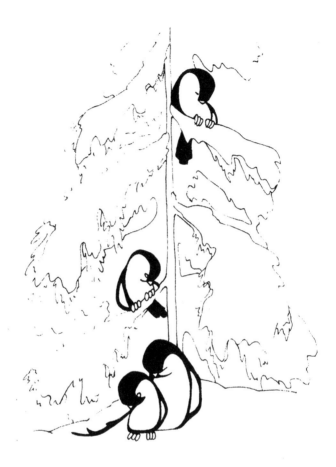

BIRDS

Kitchi-Manitou created Mother Earth and clothed her with grasses, shrubs, bushes, trees, flowers. Next were insects. Some said that it was the partridge that was first brought into being to give birth and to be the Mother of all birds that made their homes in the forests, meadows and lakes.

As the birds came to life, Kitchi-Manitou sent them to every part of Mother Earth to look after her clothing, to carry the seeds of life for flowers and plants and to bring music to animals and humans.

To each species Kitchi-Manitou gave a territory to look after, seeds to sow, insects to control. The birds were not given outright ownership of the territory that they were assigned; only tenancy.

Right from the beginning the crane and the loon were chosen to perform special duties in Anishinaubae spiritual ceremonies. The curve of the loon's neck served as a design for the head of the drumming stick used on the water drum in the Medaewaewin ceremony. In a mystical way the loon's neck image would lend the magic of its call to the sound of the drum, inviting people to the service and summoning the manitous to bestow their favours upon the petitioners.

The loon earned its special place and standing in Anishinaubae Medaewaewin rituals in the following manner.

Seven grandfathers were appointed to preside over the Anishinaubae peoples. But they were too distant from the earth and from human life to pass their knowledge to men and women. It was more likely that humans would listen to one of their own kind who lived in their midst.

They then sent one of their couriers to look for a worthy candidate whom they would instruct and who would live by the teachings, and in turn pass the lessons on to others. Six times the courier went around the earth without finding anyone. On the seventh search the courier took a new-born child from its parents and brought it back to the seven grandfathers.

Too young to understand the spirit world, the child had first to learn about and understand the world. To prepare the child for learning about the life of the spirit and soul, the courier took him around the earth and among the stars. Seven years later the courier brought the child, now a boy, back to the grandfathers.

Until he reached manhood, the grandfathers taught the boy what he needed to know about life and living. When they completed their instructions, they gave the man a large bundle. The man didn't know his way back home. To show the man the way home, the grandfathers persuaded an otter to suspend its play and to escort the man to his home. Near the man's village the otter went back to his play, leaving the man to complete his journey home alone.

When the old man got back to his village he distributed the gifts of wisdom and learning and the knowledge of the Great Laws that he had received from the grandfathers to guide the Anishinaubae peoples in living by the codes. The old man chose a young boy as his apprentice who, when he had learned what he needed to know about life, would pass these precepts on to others.

Not long into his apprenticeship the boy took sick. No one, not even the old man knew what to do to save the boy from death. Everyone expected the worst. Whippoorwills keened, loons wailed.

The old man, not knowing what to do, turned to the grandfathers for help.

He made a water drum according to the one that the grandfathers had shown him in a dream. The drum's beat and echo were the music and talk that the grandfathers listened to. As for the echo-maker, the old man designed its head with a curve to resemble the curve of the loon's neck. The echo of the drum wailed across the sky and drew the attention of the grandfathers.

The grandfathers and the manitous came later that day. First they taught the old man that plants and trees and their parts were not only food but medicine as well. After teaching the old man, they brought the sick boy back to health.

The loon still wails to this day for its young, for its mate, for the sick, for the people.

As well as serving in the Medaewaewin ceremonies as a spiritual symbol, the loon is an avenger.

A woman whose children had run away across the St. Mary's River at Sault Ste. Marie asked a crane to carry her across the river. The crane had been resting and nursing its head wound from a recent fight with another crane. Still weak from the loss of blood, and its scars now yet fully healed, the crane hesitated. He told the woman about his condition but that he would carry her across only if she promised not to touch his head wounds. The woman gave her word.

High up over the river the woman saw blood oozing from the crane's head wound. Feeling sorry for the crane and wanting to staunch the flow of blood, the women touched the crane's head to wipe the blood. The moment that she touched the bird's head, both plummeted into the rapids, where the woman was dashed to a pulp. Her remains turned into roe, the roe into whitefish.

In the spring the following year a large whitefish had just given birth to a large brood of little baby whitefish. Soon after, the minnows were at play in the shallows, just below the surface of the waters.

Later the mother whitefish swam to the shallows to see that her offspring were safe, just as a loon was teaching her own offspring how to dive and how to stay under water for as long as they could. The mother loon was coaching her youngsters long distance diving. As each of the little loons surpassed the previous mark, the mother loon moved the marker a little further off.

And, for bettering their latest dive, mother loon awarded the contestant a whitefish minnow.

The whitefish protested, "You're killing my children. You'll kill all of us! What have you got against us?"

"You'd overrun our home if we didn't keep you in check," the loon replied. "Besides ... you killed our kin, the crane!"

Before Nana'b'oozoo left the land of the Anishinaubaek, heartbroken by neglect, loons used to travel and congregate in great flocks like geese. After Nana'b'oozoo and his grandmother left the land and their neighbours, unnoticed and unmourned, the loons, the only ones to miss him and the old lady, separated and went about in pairs, searching for Nana'b'oozoo. They went about the lakes looking for something that was missing that was once a part of their lives. If men and women didn't care that Nana'b'oozoo was gone from life, then the loons would search for and invite him to return, if not to the people, then at least to the world of loons.

And so the loons took the lead in searching for the Anishinaubae people's brother and in bringing him back to the way of life that Nana'b'oozoo once exemplified. The loons searched the skies, they flew over the tree tops, they skimmed the water's surface, they set up watch in coves and inlets, they probed the depths of lakes where they asked the fish if any one of them had seen Nana'b'oozoo. They searched in pairs, always within hearing distance of each other.

They keen as parents do, when they lose a child.
They cry as women, when they lose a mate.
They wail in fear, lest they lose each other.
They lament that their offspring may never know
A heritage that they shared with the Anishinaubae people.
They call each other
"Stay near,
You are all that I have."

After the Great Flood, Kitchi-Manitou made Great Laws for humans, birds, animals to live by to enable them to live in harmony with the earth and with themselves. Kitchi-Manitou also gave all living creatures duties to fulfill for the earth, for each other, and rituals to perform.

As the years went by people began to violate the Great Laws. They thought more and more about themselves than they did about others. Hunters spent more time fighting to gain honours than working to feed their families. They conducted rituals and asked the manitous to help them gain what they sought for themselves. They let selfishness, which they were to master, instead master them.

In their selfishness, humans flouted the Great Laws of Kitchi-Manitou. Displeased, Kitchi-Manitou called a courier and gave him instructions to punish humans.

An eagle, soaring high above the clouds between the earth and the star world, overheard Kitchi-Manitou's instructions. The eagle flew directly to Kitchi-Manitou and asked the Master of Life to spare humans. Kitchi-Manitou granted the eagle's request on condition that the eagle find at least one man or woman who still lived by the Great Laws and performed the rituals not for personal gain but for the good of everyone. The eagle was required to report to Kitchi-Manitou every day if there were people abiding by the Laws.

Every day at dawn the eagle ascends into the sky to keep watch upon the people below. From its lookout the eagle can see whatever evil that humans do; it can also see much good. On seeing good, the eagle reports it to Kitchi-Manitou.

Human beings owe more to the eagle than they realize. Its feathers are used in some ceremonies; feathers are emblems of courage and foresight and wisdom.

HOW THE BIRDS GOT THEIR COLOURS

The birds sitting on the edge of an escarpment were watching a procession of animals down below them in a valley.

After watching the parade for some time without a word, the Jay finally broke the silence. He said to his companions, the Eagle, the Crow and the Seagull, "Look at them. Don't you think that they look dapper? Wouldn't you like a coat like they have?"

The Eagle, the Crow and the Seagull said nothing.

A little later the Jay added, "I'd give anything to have a coat like that."

"Like what?" the Crow asked.

"Like that black and white striped coat with the bushy tail up in the air."

"Humph!" the Crow sniffed. "I don't see anything special about that coat. The owner is so stuck up, as if she were somebody. If she only knew how much she smelled, she wouldn't walk around with her nose and tail so high up in the air. Her neighbours and kin say that she doesn't wash, and that's the reason she has no friends."

"I know nothing about that" the Jay said. "It has nothing to do with the coat. It is still a fine coat.... I also like that coat that fat animal is wearing."

"Which one?"

"The one wearing a black band across her eyes and black rings around her tail, with a train of kids behind her like a 'possum."

"You mean Raccoon. Cleanliness herself? Do you know why she's always washing her hands?"

When the Jay shook his head the Crow continued, "It's because she's always in someone's garbage; she gets her hands dirty, like a regular thief ... and ... her children are just like her. When they're around, even their kin have to keep things locked up."

The Jay didn't say another word, but the Crow kept up a steady chatter, gossiping about this animal, now that one. There was no one like that old Crow for finding fault or, if he didn't find one, he invented one. He couldn't say anything good about anyone.

For his part the Jay paid no more attention to the Crow; instead he concentrated on the parade. And as he gazed on the column of animals, the Jay was transfixed as the difference between the coating of animals and birds sank into his mind. Compared to the coats of the animals, those of the birds were plain, homely. Crows, ravens, eagles, hawks, thrushes, sparrows, gulls, ducks, geese, partridges, swallows, wrens were all white. No one could tell them apart at once. They themselves had to look at least twice before they could recognize friend, kin or neighbour.

As the Jay saw it, the animals didn't deserve coats that were more colourful than those of the birds. The birds were much more graceful, made music with their voices, and travelled on land, sea and air at speeds that the animals could never match. It wasn't fair that these clumsy, slow, dim-witted, plain creatures had such colourful coats. The birds had been fleeced; they too should have had beautiful coats. Just the thought of nature's forgetfulness made the Jay scowl, but he was also very envious, and growing discontented, bitter.

The Jay sounded out the Eagle. "I wish I had your good looks," he said. "You have strength, grace, dignity, courage, confidence. You must surely be one of the handsomest beings in all of creation. I have yet to see an animal to compare.... It's a pity you don't have a better, a more colourful coat."

The Eagle had never thought about his appearance. The Jay must be right, for he didn't lie. At least he was right about his coat. It was plain. Why, even the humblest of animals had a more distinctive coat. Why not he? He was cheated. It wasn't right. In a sour mood, the Eagle snapped his beak and curled his talons.

Together the Jay and the Eagle discussed what should be done. They agreed that it would be easier to get new coats or have their old one's dyed if only all, or most, of the birds wanted the same thing. So agreed, they set to work at once, pointing out to their nearest neighbours, the Seagull and the Crow, how nature had played favourites by giving coloured coats to the animals but not to the birds. All were created equal, were they not? They deserved to be as well clad as their brothers, the animals, did they not? This inequality had to be set right.

The Seagull and the Crow agreed that something had to be done. They would do whatever the Jay and the Eagle advised. Spread the word was the advice. Along with the Jay and the Eagle, the Seagull and the Crow stirred up four of their neighbours by drawing attention to nature's uneven handout of coloured coats. Word spread quickly, and in no time the birds were grumbling in resentment.

"Where? How? When?" the disgruntled birds demanded. Neither the Jay nor the Eagle knew. The Jay flew down and asked one of the animals passing by where he had got his beautiful coloured coat. "From Pukawiss," the Muskrat replied. And he also asked the Muskrat where he and all his companions were going. According to the Muskrat, he and his kind were invited to a festival by Pukawiss.

Back on the escarpment the Jay relayed the news that he had gathered.

The birds went straightaway to Pukawiss's lodge and asked for coloured coats. But that manitou was too busy preparing for the festival that he couldn't attend to their request right then. However, he assured the birds that he would look after them once the festival was over. In the meantime, they could stay and watch the plays and the performances.

On the day following the festival Pukawiss re-arranged the decor around his lodge. When the birds awakened there was already a huge tree trunk that served as a table in place; to one side on the ground were several logs placed end to end. On top of the logs were birch bark containers, Pukawiss's instruments and appliances.

Because there was so much pushing and shoving, grumbling and whining, Pukawiss had to roar out for quiet and order. When the din had subsided, Pukawiss directed the birds to line up and bade them to choose a colour or colours from the containers as they came to the front in their turns.

A line was formed. Most of the birds wanted to be in the forefront, except for the Jay, the Eagle, the Seagull and the Crow, who ran to the back of the line. From the back they could see what colours and designs their kin chose, and then dream up a better one.

When the first bird in line was called forward to choose a colour or any combination of colours, he walked back and forth, back and forth, peering into the containers, quite unable to make up his mind. Naturally, the other birds grew impatient and demanded that he hurry or go to the back.

Finally the little bird decided, and took his place atop the tree trunk. Pukawiss took the two containers chosen by the bird and set them down on his makeshift table. Then he took out a small feather brush and dipped it into the container.

Gently, lightly, Pukawiss passed the brush over the little bird's head, back, tail and around the bird's closed eyes.

"Yellow! Yellow!" the other birds exclaimed, and they craned and stretched their necks to get a better look still.

The word "Yellow! Yellow!" went from bird to bird to the end of the line.

Afraid to miss something, the birds kept their eyes riveted on the artist and his model. They watched silently as Pukawiss made his model stand first on one leg and then on the other so that he could paint the bird's undercarriage.

When Pukawiss finished painting the little bird's coat, he asked the bird to spread its wings. With another brush which he dipped in another container, Pukawiss dabbed the wings.

"Black! Black wings!" the spectators cried.

The little bird examined himself, twisting and turning to see his sides and his back, looking from side to side to inspect his outstretched wings, and bending almost upside down to look between his legs at his underside.

Delighted with his appearance, the little yellow bird with black wings gave thanks to Pukawiss. Taking the little bird in his hand, Pukawiss threw him up into the skies.

Every head was turned upward to gaze at the beautiful goldfinch.

"Humph!" the Crow sniffed. "Just two colours! Yellow! Black! Yech! When my turn comes, I'm going to choose all the colours. I want a coat of many colours. A polka dot coat."

Like all their kin the Jay, the Eagle, the Seagull and the Crow took a keen interest in the artist's work. While bird after bird took its place on the table, with a few gentle strokes Pukawiss changed the plain coats of birds into red, blue, green, brown, grey, indigo, orange, buff, and into two-three-four toned birds, and mottled and spotted ones. By magic and medicine, Pukawiss changed something ordinary and common into something beautiful and fetching. Now the birds were even more beautiful than were the animals.

The line of birds moved forward steadily, growing shorter.

Only once was Pukawiss interrupted in his work.

He had said "Next!" Then he asked in surprise, "And who are you?" as he looked down.

"The animals call me a bat," the little voice said. "They say I'm a bird because I have wings, I fly and I eat bugs. They don't want me in their company. I'd rather be a bird anyway. I don't want to be an animal ... they're gross."

"But he's not a bird" an old Buzzard objected. "He's got no feathers ... and a bird must have feathers. Besides, he's got fur like a rat, ears like a rat, and teeth like a rat. He doesn't belong with us."

"You see, nobody wants me," the little bat complained, almost crying.

Feeling sorry for the little outcast, Pukawiss dabbed some grey and black on him. Before he let the bat go, Pukawiss whispered to him, "You can be a bird at night, and a little animal during the day."

Meanwhile the goodwill between the Jay, the Eagle, the Seagull and the Crow was going downhill. At first there was a lot of good natured bantering and nudging. But as they drew closer to the front, their tones got sharper and their prods more forceful and sudden.

Now it was the Crow who undid the goodwill. As the line grew shorter the Crow wanted more than before to be the last in line. By being at the very end he would be able to choose colours and patterns that were brighter than any chosen by all the other birds. To gain the very last spot the Crow tried cunning to distract his companions and, while the other three were off guard, he would run to the rear. For instance, the Crow would point to someone or something and, while his companions' attention was directed elsewhere, he would claim the last. Twice he kicked the Jay and then blamed the Seagull. The Eagle had to pull the Jay and the Seagull apart to restore peace. When order was restored, the Crow was behind them all.

Exasperated by the Crow's shenanigans, the Eagle sat on him, as a hen sits on her chicks.

But the Jay and the Seagull continued their squabbling and skirmishing. Neither one noticed that they were, along with the Eagle and the Crow, the last four birds. In fact, not one of the four noticed that they were at the front until Pukawiss seized the Jay by the neck saying "You're next."

After the Jay, the Seagull was next.

From under the Eagle, the Crow snorted as he made fun of the Seagull. "Gray! ... On his back ... the rest ... white. What a dimwit! He's got no colour sense whatsoever. He should've gone to the front for all the good staying at the back did him." The next instant the Crow bawled out,

"Eeeeeyowh! You're hurting me; NOT SO HARD!"

The Eagle let up and allowed the Crow to go free. The Crow dusted himself and checked to see if he had any broken bones or was bleeding. Then without warning the Crow sprang on the startled Eagle. He hammered at the Eagle's head. Feathers flew as the Crow chipped away.

The Eagle recovered from the surprise attack quite quickly and with a sudden twist had the Crow on the ground. But before the Eagle could injure the Crow, Pukawiss grabbed the Eagle. "You're next" he said.

Last at last. The Crow was last and he smiled and strutted back and forth. He watched.

"Brown!" he scoffed. "Brown! Haw-haw-haw. White on the head. Haw-haw-haw. You're now bald-headed." And the Crow chortled.

Before taking flight the Eagle smirked and taunted the Crow. "See if you can do better."

The Crow stepped forward and leaped on top of the table. "I want all the colours," he said. "Polka dots of different sizes." And he stood waiting.

Pukawiss seized the Crow by the legs. He dipped his brush into a container and smeared the Crow with swift careless strokes.

"Caw! (which means No). Caw! Caw!" the Crow croaked in alarm. "I said I want all the colours."

But Pukawiss continued to smear the Crow with black dye.

"Caw! Caw! Caw! Didn't you hear? I said all the colours, not just black!"

Not far above the Eagle floated gently in circles, as if held up by an invisible hand. Pukawiss sloshed the paint on, heedless of the Crow's protests, commanding him to hold still.

"Caw! Caw! Caw! No! No! No! I want all the colours. Polka dot design." And the Crow squirmed and wiggled to get away.

"But black is all I've got left," Pukawiss explained, and he threw the Crow up into the air. "I don't have any other kind."

"Hee, hee, hee, hee!" the Eagle cackled in glee. "Your taste and colour sense is no better than the Seagull. Ha! Ha! Ha!"

The Crow was in instant pursuit, ready to pluck the Eagle alive. It was only because the Eagle had a long head start that he escaped, otherwise he would have been knocked down in mid-flight.

The Crow never forgave the Eagle for sitting on him and for laughing at his misfortune. Every chance he got the Crow took off after the Eagle, meaning to do him in. And it is still so to this day.

ROBINS — Few birds are as close to the Anishinaubae people as are robins. And there is a good reason for this.

The robin was once a boy who wanted to be a chanter to fulfill his dream, but his father wouldn't hear of such useless occupation. The son should aspire to become a hunter to serve his family and community in a useful way.

Not to be allowed to become a chanter was more than the boy could bear. He wanted to make his father happy, but he also wanted to be happy.

During a vision quest the little boy dreamed of a bright orange fire over which was a dark cloud. He burned in the fire.

Later, when his father came to fetch him, the boy, now transformed into a robin, spoke to his father, but his father didn't hear him. He watched his father look around and call for him, and then sit down and weep. The robin warbled to cheer up his father.

Eventually the father fell asleep. He dreamed. In his dream his son came to him, as a boy then as a robin.

"Father!" the boy spoke to his father. "I love you. Ever since I was a child I wanted to make music, to make you and people happy. As a boy I could not do that. Now as a robin, I can. From now on I and my descendants will sing for you."

The man's dream ended. When he awakened, sad, he heard his son sing and whistle to him as a robin, trying to console and cheer him up. When the man went home, the robin followed, settling on a tree near the man's home.

That robin's descendants still make music for men and women

and children, in snow, rain, heat and cold, and make their nests near human's homes.

WOODPECKERS — As the robin was once a boy, so was the woodpecker once a woman. It was as a robin that a boy fulfilled his dream to become a chanter. To protect trees and eat insects and grubs was not what the old woman wanted, but it was a fate that she deserved for her selfishness.

The woodpecker serves and protects trees. It also exemplifies a lesson that selfishness deserves to be punished.

THE OLD WOMAN BECOMES A WOODPECKER — While the old woman was kneading yet another roll of dough, she saw a man in the distance walking toward her. She didn't need to look twice; she knew who he was. Of all people to come, especially when she was cooking, there was none worse that this old creep. For sure he'd be hungry and expect to be fed.

Frantically she ran back and forth between fireplace and her wigwaum, hiding the pile of breads that she had baked. Old bums like the old man didn't deserve a handout. All he did was go from place to place, from home to home, begging for meals or small scraps of food. If only he'd work, hunt and fish like other men, he wouldn't have to beg. For sure he'd say that he had not had anything to eat for days. If she could help it, she wouldn't give him a crumb, no matter how much he begged. She didn't work hard baking bread just to feed old beggars. Well, maybe a bun.

The old man was Nanabush, and he breathed in deeply to smell the bread as he drew nearer the old woman's wigwaum. My, the bread smelled good, but better still, it meant that he would soon eat. Now Nanabush did not need to smell the bread to know that the old woman was cooking. Just by looking at the blaze in the fireplace and the pile of firewood Nanabush could tell that she was cooking something. Besides, he could see flour on the old woman's dress and hands. And Nanabush breathed a sigh of relief, anticipating an invitation to eat.

Cheerfully he greeted the old woman, "Ahneen, mindemoyaehn!

(Hello, old lady!). I couldn't have timed my arrival any better. I'm just on time. I could smell your bread even before I saw your wigwaum. You must be a marvellous cook. I don't think I've smelled better bread."

Nanabush put his bag down and set his bow and arrows to one side. The old lady ground her teeth to stifle her annoyance with this unwanted visit.

"I must ask your kindness," the old man said, just as she knew he would. "I've been hunting for days, and I haven't seen so much as a rabbit. I don't understand where all the animals and birds have gone. They disappeared just like that. Now I'm tired and hungry. I don't think I can go much further. I'm not asking for much; no more than a crust of bread; that's all I need. It would be quite enough to get me home."

"Goodness!" the old woman almost gasped. "Just by asking me for a crust reminds me how poor I am. Do you know how poor I am? I'm poorer than poor."

"Kitchi-manitou will look after your needs for your kindness," Nanabush promised the old woman. "The Great Creator will not forget you. I, myself, will bring you meat the next time I kill a deer."

"Look! This is all I have," the old woman said, and she held out a ball of dough the size of an apple. "I'll give you half," she added, breaking the dough in half and placing it near the fire.

Weary from hunting and weak from hunger, Nanabush settled on the ground and in an instant fell asleep. Meanwhile, the woman tended the bread. As she watched that it not burn or fall into the flames, the dough swelled and swelled until it was the size of a large pumpkin and brown as brown could be. The old woman's eyes grew wide in wonder as she watched the bread. Then they narrowed as she looked at her unwanted guest. Why should she share her good fortune with this old beggar? She hid the loaf in the wigwaum.

From the little ball of dough that remained, the old woman broke off another piece, rolled it between the palms of her hands before placing it on the rock near the flames. Again the same thing happened. That little dough puffed up like a mushroom in the rain until it was as large as a pumpkin. It shouldn't have grown so much but it did, and she couldn't understand why. It must be the doings of the manitous. And the more the old woman looked at and thought about the bread, the less she wanted to share it with the old beggar sleeping on the ground. It was much too good, too big for the old man. A crust was all he deserved and asked for. If that was all he wanted, that is all he would receive; not a whole loaf. The old woman removed the loaf from the fireplace and hid it in her wigwaum along with the other loaves, slipping out so quietly that her visitor neither saw nor heard her.

She then took what was left of the dough, a morsel no bigger than an acorn, and set it near the flames. As if by magic, that tiny knot of dough grew and grew. Only when it was as large as a pumpkin did it stop growing. Besides, it was a rich brown. It was much too big and to brown to part with. Quickly and quietly the old woman hid the loaf in her wigwaum before her visitor woke up.

But soon afterward Nanabush woke up. "Have you a crust of bread for me?" he asked.

"Ooooooooooh!" the old woman wailed. "I had a terrible accident while I was baking your bread.... Your bread ... and mine, fell into the fire; and ... I'm sorry ... I have nothing else to offer you."

The old man jumped to his feet, glared at the old woman before snarling, "You lie; you lie because you are nothing but a stingy, selfish old person. You lie because you care only about yourself; you don't care about anybody else. If that's the case, if you care only about your belly, if you won't spare even a crust to a hungry stranger, then from this day on shall you scrounge for every meal ... for every bite. Never again will you eat a meal at one sitting or in comfort. Never again shall you taste bread or meat. Instead, you will feed upon the grubs and weevils and termites that make their homes in trees, one worm at a time. Not again will you drink water from cup or stream. From this moment on you will have to chip away at trees, not only for a single mouthful of food, but also for a drop of sap."

In that instant the old woman was changed into a woodpecker.

THE WOODPECKER AND THE WORM — A brother and his sister were watching a woodpecker who was halfway up a tree. To the children the bird looked as if he had lost something and was searching for it. At other times the bird appeared to be testing the tree, tapping here, now there. This was not the first time that the children had seen woodpeckers so occupied. But not until now did they bother to ask what the woodpecker was doing.

The first question they asked was why the woodpecker was drumming at the tree. Other questions followed. Why was the woodpecker trying to knock the tree down? Why didn't the stupid bird start at the bottom, as did human beings? How long would it take a woodpecker to hew down a tree? Wouldn't the woodpecker break or blunt its beak? What happens if the woodpecker breaks its beak? If it merely blunted its beak, how does a woodpecker sharpen it? Don't the chips fly into the woodpecker's eye? ... and how do they drink?

There was only one person who would know the answers to their questions, their grandmother. Noko! They went directly to her.

"Noko! Why does a woodpecker want to hew down a tree?"

"Now! What gave you the idea that a woodpecker was knocking down a tree?"

"Well, we saw one chopping away and we saw chips falling," they explained.

"I suppose woodpeckers look as if they're hewing trees, but they are not really doing that. Actually, they are eating."

"EATING!" the grandchildren were astonished. "What could they possibly find on the sides of trees worth eating?"

"Manitoushuk! (insects, weevils, bugs, any little creature that infests trees)," their grandmother explained. "Let's go back out and watch. Where is the woodpecker?"

The grandchildren led her to the place where they had seen the woodpecker.

She explained, "Watch! Watch how careful she is, as she goes about the side of the tree! Watch how closely she looks over the surface of the tree; all around, above and below, from right to left. Watch how she studies the ridges and the hollows in the bark of the tree. Watch how she tests the surface of the bark itself ... tap ... tap, tap ... tap ... tap; not hard, not fast, as if she might injure or break the bark. Watch how she rests in her search. Watch how she inclines her head first to one side and then to the other. Watch! Watch how she goes through the same motions after she tests the bark."

"The bird that you see used to be an old woman who was turned into a woodpecker by Nanabush for her selfishness. And since that time she has had to scrounge for her food, nits and grubs within the tree. In scrounging even for the smallest of these bugs, the woodpecker must take care not to frighten the nits and ticks, grubs and weevils. Otherwise she won't have a bite to eat.

If her behaviour is quaint, it is because she is exercising good manners; and, were you to hear the conversation between the woodpecker and either a nit or a tick within the tree, this is what you are likely to hear.

Tap, tap, tap ... tap, tap.

'Ahneen manitoush ... Hello Worm! Are you there?'

'Ahneen Paupaussae ... Hello Woodpecker! What do you want?' The worm is as polite as is the woodpecker ... and talkative. My, she likes to talk. Once she starts, she can't stop. 'Ahneen Paupaussae! Is there anything that I can do for you?'

Meanwhile, the woodpecker is looking all around, listening. She taps again.

Tap ... tap ... tap ... tap, tap.

'Ahneen manitoush! Did I wake you up?'

'Tauhau Paupaussae! Of course not. Were you expecting me to be still asleep ... in bed? Ha, ha, ha! I've been awake since dawn. Do you think I'm lazy?' My the worm likes to talk, gets carried away by words.

Meanwhile the woodpecker is looking all around, listening. She taps again.

Tap, tap, tap ... tap, tap.

'Ahneen manitoush! Am I knocking too hard upon your house?'

'Tauhau Paupaussae! Really now! My friend! Knock too hard? You can knock as hard and as long as your head can stand it, you'll never shake my house. Maybe you'll shiver your beak before you shiver me timbers! Ha, ha, ha, ha.'

Meanwhile the woodpecker is looking all around, listening. Then she taps again.

Tap ... tap, tap ... tap, tap.

'Ahneen manitoush! If you don't like my hammering, tell me and I'll go away.'

'No! No! No! Please don't go. You're not disturbing me at all.' My, that little worm loved to talk. 'Whatever you're doing sounded like drumming to me. I thought you were testing a new drum, trying out a new beat. Please drum some more ... a little faster. I like music; it makes me feel like dancing....'

Meanwhile the woodpecker is looking all around, listening. She taps once more.

Tap, tap, tap, tap, tap, tappity, tappity, tap.

'I'm coming out to dance ... faster ... don't stop.'

Watch! See how pleased the woodpecker looks. If she leaves and makes directly for the base of a cedar or a birch, it means that the woodpecker has got the worm and must now moisten her throat with sap in order to swallow her meal.

Take a look at cedars and birches. You will find a ring of holes at the base of some of these trees. They are watering holes where woodpeckers drink.

Watch! Watch that woodpecker. When she finishes sipping a drop of sap, she will return to her feeding place. Watch how she goes through the same motions, all for a crumb, less than a mouthful at a time.

BUZZARDS — Birds and animals die, leave their corpses and bones to litter and clutter up the forests and meadows. Yet the forests and meadows are remarkably clean.

Credit for keeping the forests and meadows clean and tidy is due to the work of an army of cleaners and janitors: flies, ants, butterflies, worms and, of course, birds.

Chief among the birds that keep the earth preened and primped are the buzzards and their kin; the seagulls and their kin.

Buzzards and vultures perch on rotten limbs on rotting trees waiting for something to die. They are unkempt, disheveled. If nothing dies, they starve to death.

Several buzzards were perched on top of a dead tree watching Nana'b'oozoo roasting a deer that he had just killed. They drooled and slobbered as they sniffed the aroma of cooking deer meat. They clacked and clicked their beaks as if they could already taste the meat. As they looked on, each of them hoped that Nana'b'oozoo would soon so stuff himself that he would go to sleep and then they would help themselves to the leftovers. A young buzzard who didn't know any better asked an older buzzard to speak to the man and ask him to share some of the meat with them.

"Hmmmmph!" grunted the old buzzard. "A waste of your breath. You may as well ask a tree to grow apples in the winter. That skinflint wouldn't give you a bone even if you were starving."

"What will we do then? How will we get our share? I'm so hungry, so weak I can hardly stand. I can't last much longer."

"Patience my boy! Just wait! When Nana'b'oozoo has bloated himself, he'll go to sleep. Then we'll help ourselves."

"Don't be so sure" a third old buzzard grumbled. "That old seagull is just like Weendigo, and he can even out eat that glutton any time. He never leaves anything for others, or for his own tomorrow."

"What will we do?" the young buzzard wailed.

"Distract him. Take his mind and his attention off his meal. He's easily distracted and upset. All we need do is to think of something that will keep Nana'b'oozoo from enjoying his meal. If we can do that, Nana'b'oozoo will forget his meal and leave it to get rid of the annoyance. Then we can help ourselves. Now think of something!"

The buzzards thought, drooled and gulped as they thought. Another youthful buzzard was all for sending a swarm of blackflies to drive Nana'b'oozoo into shelter or into making a smudge fire and standing in the safety of the smoke. The idea was good, the older buzzards said, but it was too late in the season for blackflies. A second young buzzard suggested that they call the Thunderbirds to create a storm with lightning and thunder and drive Nana'b'oozoo into hiding. Good as the idea was, the older buzzards pointed out that they too would have to stay in some shelter. But for all their thinking, the buzzards could not come up with an idea that would lure or drive Nana'b'oozoo away from his meal long enough for the buzzards to fly in to steal a bite.

They could only watch and clack their beaks in envy. Nor did they dare ask.

Nana'b'oozoo, of course, noticed the buzzards watching him.

"Buzz off!" he growled. "Get your own meal, you lazy good for nothings. Beggars! Beat it before I put an arrow through your rotten gizzards. Go on! You're letting everyone know that I've got something to eat. Go on!"

But the buzzards moved nary an inch. They knew that Nana'b'oozoo was bluffing.

Soon the North Wind began to blow, not hard but gently and steadily. The trees swayed to and fro with the wind. There were two trees that grew side by side so closely that they rubbed and dubbed, squeaked and scraped, groaned and ground, grated and rasped.

At the foot of the trees, Nana'b'oozoo looked up and glared. After a moment he took his eyes off the trees and bit angrily into a piece of meat he held in his hand. In the next breath he stopped chewing and glowered as if he could scare the trees into keeping quiet.

But the trees continued to squeak and scrape and rasp.

Nana'b'oozoo scowled even harder, his eyes like burning embers and his face hard as flint and ice.

"QUIET! ENOUGH!" Nana'b'oozoo roared at the trees. "You're making too much noise. Don't you know enough when to stop!? You're disturbing the forest and everyone in it. We've had enough! I want to eat in peace... to enjoy my meal."

The trees rubbed and scrubbed, groaned and ground, squeaked and scraped, rasped and grated.

"DIDN'T YOU HEAR!?" Nana'b'oozoo bellowed even louder than before. If you don't stop now, I'll cut you down and use you for kindling." But the trees paid no heed. They rubbed and groaned, scraped and grated.

Nana'b'oozoo couldn't stand it any longer. He dropped the meat that he had been eating. He sprang to his feet and, like a mad, wounded bear, charged the two birch trees that were leaning against each other and creating the disturbance. Nana'b'oozoo shimmied up one tree until he came to the place where the birches were rubbing. He pried them apart and squeezed himself between. Then with all his strength he held them apart at arms' length. But within moments Nana'b'oozoo weakened and the trees closed on him like a trap. They wedged Nana'b'oozoo between them so that he couldn't move. It was all he could do to keep the trees from crushing him.

Nana'b'oozoo was caught fast. He was gasping for breath. He called to the buzzards. "My friends! Help me! I'm caught! The trees won't let me go! I'm being crushed!" and Nana'b'oozoo wheezed.

But the buzzards said not a word. It was as if they were deaf. "My brothers!" Nana'b'oozoo pleaded. "Please have pity! Help me before I'm crushed. If you help me, I'll return the favour some day." Nana'b'oozoo wheezed some more.

But the buzzards cast not even a glance his way. They kept their eyes on the meat on the ground. They drooled and they slobbered. A feast for the taking.

Down they drifted, alighting on the remains of Nana'b'oozoo's meal. They ripped and gouged the meat from the bones, clicked and clacked their beaks as men and women smacked their lips.

Even before the buzzards dug their beaks into the roast a third time there was a roar, "Scram you scum! Charge, boys!" And there followed yips and yelps, growls and snarls as a pack of wolves raced into the midst of the buzzards.

At the first outcry the buzzards squawked and flapped their wings and beat the air to get away from the snapping fangs of the wolves. Feathers flew as the wolves nipped the wings and tails of the birds, but the buzzards got away. They flew to the treetops, sweating and breathing heavily.

Meanwhile, the wolves settled down and feasted, tearing the meat from the bones until only some gristle and fragments of meat and fur were left.

While the wolves ate, Nana'b'oozoo gasped, "It's mine! Mine! Leave it alone! Wait till I get my hands on you! I'll tear you apart with my own hands and give the pieces to the seagulls!" But the wolves didn't hear. Nana'b'oozoo might as well have shouted to the wind. He only got weaker.

After the wolves had eaten their fill and could eat no more, they laid down to sleep beside what remained of the deer.

Up in the tree Nana'b'oozoo no longer thought about his meal. He thought only of his life now.

"Someone! Anyone! Help me!" Nana'b'oozoo gasped.

A rush of wind tore through the forest. It whipped one of the birches to one side before the tree snapped back against the other birch. But that one instant was enough to set Nana'b'oozoo loose and send him tumbling to the ground, knocking the wind out of him. When Nana'b'oozoo came to his senses and opened his eyes, the limbs and branches, and the buzzards perched on them were spinning around him as if they were on a merry-go-round. Nana'b'oozoo closed his eyes. He thought that he was going to get sick.

A little later he opened his eyes again. This time the trees weren't going around in circles. The buzzards were still there.

Nana'b'oozoo sat up. He shook his fist at the buzzards. "You scabs! Scum! Slobs! Good for nothings! All you do is wait to steal food. Wait and watch and stand by and do nothing to help a neighbour. Just waited for me to die so that you could help yourselves to my food. But I fooled you, didn't I?

For not lifting a hand to help me when I called you, for wanting me dead so that you could have my food, I'm going to make you pay! Never again will you hunt and kill as do eagles and hawks. You'll eat what wolves, foxes, wolverines, ravens and crows leave. You'll eat rotten stinking flesh and dead meat and decaying fish. You'll never have peace of mind. You'll never know whether you'll live to see tomorrow. You won't be able to kill, and if nothing dies, you'll die.

And for being lazy, for being unwilling to work for your own food, you will never again know rest. You will clean up the litter and the waste left by humans, birds and animals. You will keep Mother Earth clean and tidy."

And so it is.

SEAGULLS — Seagulls are grace and beauty in form and in motion, but within their hearts and souls dwells a spiteful spirit.

> The birds, animals and insects
> Call out
> Watch! Listen!
> That you be not beguiled.
> Grace and beauty
> May hide
> A spirit mean.

After he had opened his gift package and distributed raspberries to the crowd of birds, animals, insects and fish, the bear growled at the beaver, "Your turn. THE BEAVER IS NEXT! QUIET!" he thundered.

The beaver, too nervous, perhaps too anxious, fumbled with the lid; the box slipped from his grasp and fell to the ground. There was a gentle, pleasant, gushing sound.

Almost crying because he had dropped his box, the beaver bent down to recover the contents of his box. His voice choked as beaver explained, "It feels soft ... it is soft...." He tasted it and declared, "It is sweet, ... refreshing. It shall be called water."

The pleasant, gentle gushing sound made its way along the ground at the feet of all present and into the distance, into the unknown. And the beaver invited all his neighbours to try the "water."

There was now no holding back by anyone. Everyone wanted to be next. It was now a question of keeping order and it was the bear who brought order out of the confusion by appointing who was to be next in the course.

From time to time the bear's voice boomed out in the darkness. "Next! ... QUIET!" Hundreds, thousands of gifts were exchanged in the dark: berries, fruit, nuts, plants, flowers, vegetables, melons, tubers and some unusual gifts such as thorns and thistles.

Standing together to one side during this entire time and exchange of gifts were the Jay, the Raven and the Seagull. The Jay had already opened his gift and had shared his acorns; so too had the Raven who had offered his fellow beings a kind of inedible grass. The Seagull held on fast to his container.

"I'm curious to know what you've got in your box," the Raven hinted.

"Well," the Seagull replied. "What's it to you! I'm not opening my box."

"WHAT!" both the Jay and the Raven squalled, taken aback by the Seagull's reply. When they recovered their wits, the Raven protested. "But we shared our gifts with you! And you took whatever was offered. It's only fair that you share your gift."

"I don't care what you say! I'm not opening my gift. I'm keeping it for myself! Kitchi-Manitou gave it to me. If Kitchi-Manitou meant these gifts for everybody, why didn't the Creator simply set the gifts before everyone. And I don't remember Kitchi-Manitou saying that we were to give it away."

"But! ... But!" the Jay and the Raven objected.

"I know you," the Seagull squawked. "You're jealous. Since you gave your gift away, you now have nothing left. You wasted your gift, now you want mine. I'm keeping mine," and the Seagull pressed his container still closer to his body and stepped a few paces away from the Jay and the Raven.

When the Jay and the Raven at last got over their shock, the Jay cackled as quietly as he could to the Raven, "Have you ever heard of such a thing? Have you every imagined that such a being could exist? There is not another being on the face of the earth as selfish as that Seagull. I'll wager that he'd let his own mother die rather than give her a morsel of food."

"What should be done with such a creature?"

"Let's make that tight-fisted old bird open his gift," the Raven croaked.

"How?" rasped the Jay, excited by the idea.

"Knock it from his grasp ... wrest it from him!"

"No. Let's not do that," the Jay objected. "Let's trick him into opening it instead."

"How?"

"Let's think." Both the Jay and the Raven wracked their brains. Moments went by, dragged on, crawled snail fashion until the Jay thought that the Raven had forgotten about the Seagull.

"Why not use thorns?"

"How?" the Raven croaked again.

"Buzz-buzz-buzz" the Jay whispered in the Raven's ear. The Raven chuckled as he listened to his companion's plan. "Wait" the Jay said. "I'll be right back."

The Jay was not long in returning; in his arms he carried two boxes of thorns. He spilled the thorns on the ground between him and the Raven.

"My friend," he said to the Seagull, "I've just found a box with something in it. Since you've not opened your box or given anything to our neighbours, I would like to give you a chance of doing something for the others. There's already talk about you; they're saying that you're stingy."

"Don't FRIEND me," the Seagull sneered. "I know what you're up to. But you can't fool me. You're not going to get me to open my box."

"Can't you think of anything else but that shabby old box? I don't care for your stinking old box. You can keep it, stuff it in your ear. I just wanted to give you a chance...."

"Ha!" the Seagull shrilled. "How very noble of you. You think that you can talk me into opening my gift with all that sweet talk about good-will. Think I'm a fool?"

"I don't want your box. Nobody'd care if you never opened your box. You can go to your grave with your box and no one will be the worse off. Now do you want to open this little box?"

"You just want my box," the Seagull said, suspicion in his voice, and he pressed it even closer and tighter to his side.

"Oh! What are you afraid of?" the Raven urged. "No one's both-ered you yet, have they? Go on!" And he pushed the Seagull toward the Jay.

The Seagull took only a few steps before he screeched, "There's something in my foot, a knife, a spear! It's burning. Someone ... help me ... please!" And he hopped around on one leg.

The Raven caught the screaming Seagull's leg and felt around the Seagull's foot until he discovered the end of the thorn sticking out. Meanwhile the Seagull was screeching and dancing about.

"Now open your box, just a little," the Raven crooned. "Only a lit-tle, and I'll pull out the big sliver."

"Nooooooo! Youooooo!"

The Raven pressed the thorn and twisted it a little.

"Oooooyoooh!" the Seagull yelped and he lifted the lid of his box a crack. It was just wide and long enough for hundreds of thousands ... millions of sparks to stream into the sky where they were welded like so many grains of light. While the beings looked up in awe and saw shapes and forms as they looked about them, the Seagull was screaming and screeching in pain, squalling at the Raven to pull out the thorn as he had promised.

"Hold still!" the Raven commanded. "Stop yelling in my ear!" Once more he thrust the thorn unexpectedly further into the Seagull's foot. The Seagull shrieked. "Open your box just a little more this time and I'll pull the sliver out."

Crying in pain the Seagull raised the lid a fraction. Out flew an orange ball. It drifted slowly into the sky and hung there. The Seagull was screaming, but no one paid attention. The beings were too busy examining what they were seeing more clearly for the first time. "Pull it out," the Seagull demanded. "I can't stand it. It hurts."

But instead of extracting the thorn, the Raven drove the sliver further, saying at the same time "Now my friend! Open your box one last time and then I'll pull out the thorn."

The Seagull had no choice; he opened his box. A ball of fire shot out the container and blazed into the sky. And there it hung, bright as fire, so that no one could look directly into its light.

With one swift motion the Raven withdrew the thorn from the Seagull's foot.

"You tricked me! You tricked me!" Seagull screeched as he took to the air and flew to the far side of a bay where he settled on a rock. Atop the rock the Seagull squawked and screeched in anger and in pain. From time to time for considerable periods he stood on one leg to relieve the pain in his foot in the other. And to this day Seagulls still frequently stand on one leg.

As an added penalty for his refusal to share his gifts, the Bear and his kin and their neighbours sentenced the Seagull to eat scraps, the entrails of raw fish and to keep the beaches clean by eating whatever carrion he finds. Even now the Seagull's descendants clash, scuffle, and brawl over putrid waste. They will not allow even one of their own kind to share in the spoils.

ANIMALS

After birds, animals were created. They were on earth long before our human ancestors appeared on the scene. And a good thing it was for our forebears, otherwise our first parents might not have survived. Animals already knew what food to eat, what the weather was going to be like, where to take shelter, how to hunt, what their neighbours were like, what the land was like. They lived by the seasons, giving birth in the spring on their return from the south or from their wintering places in caves and in dens. They altered their clothing and colours in keeping with the seasons, and they carried out their duties as given them by Kitchi-Manitou.

Animals knew more about the earth and life than humans who came after them. And they lived by earth, by the moon, the sun, by the weather and by the seasons. They lived in harmony with the changes.

Right from their beginning humans depended on animals, whom they often referred to as "our older brothers and sisters," meaning those who knew more and were stronger. It was clear that insects, birds and animals could do many things that humans could not. Some could fly, some lived in water, some were swifter, some were stronger. All of them were keener of hearing, sight, smell. Almost without exception all were more patient, resourceful, diligent in caring for their young than were humans.

Our ancestors owed their lives and what they knew of food, medicines, life and living from the animals, birds and insects. Our storytellers readily admitted humans' dependence upon deer, whitefish, geese, bees.

To show this dependency, the storytellers depict First Man (some call him Nana'b'oozoo or Ween'b'oozoo) being escorted by a wolf in his exploration of the world.

It was easy enough to teach First Man in the summer. All that First Man needed to know was which fruits and vegetables were good to eat and when they ripened, and to imitate squirrels and chipmunks in storing food for the winter. Wolf taught First Man to listen to the birds, to watch the signs in the skies, and to pay attention to the night birds to know what weather they predicted.

Winter was different. It was then that First Man had most to learn.

First Man knew little about dressing for winter or keeping warm at night. And so he had to sleep with Wolf and her cubs with them covering him. First Man complained about the odour of the cubs' tails so much that the wolf cubs withdrew their tails. Before long, First Man's teeth were chattering and his skin was shrinking in the awful cold.

"I'm cold!" he whimpered. "Would you lend me your tails as my blanket?"

First Man was only too glad to get some warmth to complain about the smell of the cubs' tails.

The cubs had their own beef. "This guy stinks!" they whispered among themselves.

Another time First Man found fault with the site for the night's shelter that Wolf had chosen. "It's too small. I can hardly breathe" he grumbled, "and besides, it's too dark."

"You can choose a place tomorrow evening then," Wolf promised.

Late next afternoon as they were passing by a hardwood bush, First Man told his escorts that the maple grove would be a good place for an overnight stay. Wolf raised her eyebrows in doubt but said nothing. The younger wolves too looked at each other in mock disbelief. Nevertheless, they made their beds, curled up, then fell asleep.

During the night a blizzard swept through the woods. The wind shrieked and whistled, driving snow before it. The wolves shivered but slept on. First Man couldn't sleep. His bones rattled, so cold was he, and he was afraid that he would freeze to death or be suffocated under a blanket of snow that the wind piled on him and his companions.

When he could stand the cold no longer, First Man awakened Wolf and told her that if he didn't get warmer, he wouldn't survive the night. He asked what they were to do.

Wolf awakened her family, explaining that they would have to move to keep First Man from becoming like a block of ice. Sleepily they grumbled that it was First Man's fault for having chosen such a bad camping site. Wolf led her family through white-outs and over snow-banks, keeping in touch with each other by hanging on to each other's tails—tail gaiting. First Man, who couldn't see and didn't have a tail, was the trailer, last in line. He clung to a wolf's tail for dear life.

Wolf led them into a cedar bush where he found shelter under a canopy of branches that were covered with snow. It was dark inside, as dark as a tent on a winter's night. Soon they were quietly sleeping, warmed by their bodies. First Man stopped quaking and drifted off to sleep. Outside the wind huffed and puffed but could not blow down the buffer of evergreen trees.

The pack and First Man made their way through the forest in aimless fashion, or so it seemed to the human, except that it wasn't as senseless as it appeared to be. Actually, Wolf and her family were at that moment pushing their way through drifts and deep snow to track down deer, Wolf was teaching her offspring how to hunt, their quarry's habits, and where to camp.

First Man couldn't understand why, with their numbers, they didn't rush into the herd of deer that was quartered in a cedar grove. And First Man asked about why they held back.

One of the pups, with the same question in mind, didn't wait for an answer. He bolted away from his companions and made straight for the herd. He acted as if he expected his brothers and sisters to follow him.

First Man and Wolf looked on.

Within a jump of the herd the wolf cub leaped, fangs bared, ready to sink them into the buck's throat. At the last moment the buck lowered his antlered head, brought it up quickly and, with a toss of his head, pitched the wolf cub into the air and sent it yelping and tumbling some steps away, where the cub twisted and groaned in pain. The herd moved off.

First Man looked on wide-eyed, speechless in awe. When he recovered his mind and his speech, First Man stammered that he thought that the wolf cub, with his speed and sharp teeth, would be more than the deer could withstand.

Wolf set First Man and the pack straight as she checked over the bruised cub for broken bones. "Never rely on speed alone. It will only earn you first injuries," she explained. She turned to her cub and said, "You'll survive. Don't be so impulsive next time! Let that be a lesson to you."

Then, to test First Man's judgment, Wolf asked him a series of questions as to which pup he thought would be the best hunter.

First Man looked over the pack.

"That one" he answered, pointing at a handsome pup with a long tail.

"No!" Wolf said with a shake of her head. "Tail's too long. It gets heavy and tires out the pup.... Besides, it picks up burrs and thistles that add to the weight and prickles the cub. Pick another one."

"That one" First Man replied, picking the pup with the loudest and sharpest howl.

"Too noisy," Wolf answered. "It will scare off our quarry. He's got to learn to keep quiet!"

First Man was embarrassed, and to spare him further embarrassment from giving more wrong answers, Wolf pointed to a nondescript pup as the one with the most promise as a hunter. "He listens, has a great deal of patience."

"Meantime he goes hungry," First Man retorted, mindful of his own hunger.

"Yes!" Wolf admitted, "but he'll live to relish a feast. He knows that alone he's no match for deer in a herd. We all know this. That is why we hunt in packs. Stalk our quarry. Harrass them until the most timid of them weakens from fright and cannot keep up with the herd but must drop behind. Then we move in.

That's the time that we eat ... no, feast."

While Wolf and her pack could go without food for days, First Man was hungry every morning and evening. He needed to eat more often, or so he believed.

First Man learned slowly. It seemed as if he were stupid. Wolf knew so much more about the weather, the forests, the birds and other animals than he did. What appeared so complicated for First Man seemed so simple for Wolf. From the way that Wolf explained things in a matter of fact sort of way, First Man was convinced that his mentor was showing him up in front of her cubs.

First Man looked forward to the day when he'd strike out on his own, no longer dependent upon Wolf for teaching him how to earn his meals, and keeping him sheltered and warm in winter. Wolf knew a great deal, but not everything. She didn't look ahead, otherwise she would have stored food away for the winter, as did chipmunks. Instead, she and her family lived from kill to kill.

If Wolf had been farsighted she would set food aside for the future and saved herself and her family unnecessary work and travel. First Man felt like telling Wolf what he thought but kept it to himself, afraid that Wolf would find some fault with it. There would come a day in the future when First Man would put the ideas that he developed in his learning days into practice, and show Wolf that he no longer needed her to teach and guide him. Meantime, First Man made up his mind to play a practical joke on his companion to show her that she didn't know everything.

The practical joke that First Man played on his friend led to Wolf's drowning and to the Great Flood in which First Man had to swim alone. Other animals saved First Man from drowning. From then on, First Man, having alienated the animals, who kept away from him, had to make his way in life on his own.

Except that First Man didn't fare as well as he thought he would.

DOGS — Before dogs befriended humans, they were like other animals living in the forests and hunting in the woods and meadows. They sometimes went with bears and wolves to hunt human beings.

At first it was fun hunting human beings just to hear them cry out and run for cover or climb trees to get out of the clutches of bears and wolves, but after a while the dogs tired of the "sport" and felt sorry for the poor human beings, who were slow, clumsy and weak. Except for a few, most animals could overtake human beings on the run; bears were much stronger, sparrows could do what humans could not do, and that is fly. Trout, beaver and ducks could out-swim and out-dive any human being.

Human beings deserved pity. They were nervous and timid, ever on the watch, ready to run like rabbits. When they saw a bear or heard a wolf, they ran and hid in caves or climbed a tree to escape. Why, they were even afraid of manitous.

But weak, slow, clumsy and timid as they were, human beings were dangerous. Most of the time they remained near their homes and drew most of what they ate by hunting and fishing. They hunted, seldom alone; mostly they hunted in packs.

Dogs were curious about these creatures and used to creep up near their villages at night and listen to and watch these funny looking beings. Unlike animals, men and women had only two legs. They had to stand straight up in order to walk, as bears sometimes did. With only two legs, the humans could not run very fast. They didn't have fur on their bodies; were hairless like babies, so that they had to wear furs to keep warm. Nor could they see or hear very well. And their offspring were helpless for years.

The dogs observed these odd looking beings at night eating meat and roots that they had cooked in the fire. They saw humans feed their offspring, and heard them bid their children to be quiet. And the dogs listened and heard the children whimper and beg for more food. "I'm hungry!" and the dogs saw the women shake their heads sadly and draw their children closer to them and answer, "there is no more." Still the children persisted, "Why? I'm hungry?" they wailed. The men put their fingers to their lips and whispered, "Shshshshshshsh! The bears and the wolves will hear you! Shshshshshshsh! Quiet!" But the children found it hard to keep back their tears. They sobbed as softly as they could, but the dogs could still hear them.

To hear the children cry, and to see them sad and thin and weak nearly broke the dogs' hearts.

"Let us do something for these poor creatures" they said. "Kitchi-Manitou must have a purpose for them. They have to live too."

"What shall we do for them?" the dogs asked.

"Let us warn the human beings when the bears and the wolves plan to go hunting for them. It's the least we can do."

"How can we?" a small dog asked, "especially when the human beings are afraid of us as well."

"All the better," an older dog explained. "They'll run and hide as soon as they hear us."

"Good idea! Let's do that then," the dogs agreed. "Let's keep our ears open!"

Not long after this, the dogs heard the bears planning a man-hunt. When the bears set out, the dogs raced ahead and barked near the village of the human beings. The moment that the women and the men heard the barks, howls and growls, the women and the children and the old people hid in caves and behind walls. The men armed themselves with torches and flaming arrows. They were ready for the bears.

When the bears saw the burning torches and the flaming arrows, they drew back and stopped in their tracks. Fire was the only thing that the bears were afraid of. Not wishing to be burned, the bears retreated out of range and let the human beings alone. From where they stood, the bears glared and roared and bared their teeth at the human beings. The bears felt cheated out of their meal. They could not understand how the human beings could have known about their plans and got ready for them.

On the way home the bears talked of nothing else but what happened, how the human beings had acted as if they already knew that the bears were on their way. Someone must have told them the bears agreed, but who?

The next time that the bears went hunting the same thing happened. The human beings were waiting with firebrands and flaming arrows. The bears had to retreat and return home without having anything to eat. The bears were even angrier than before. Now they were sure that someone was warning the humans.

To find out who was warning their enemies, the bears asked the wolves to keep an eye out for anyone who might be telling the humans about the bears' plans and undo all the bears' hard work. The bears let the wolves know that they were going on a hunt the very next day.

Even before the sun was up the wolves were on their way, well in advance of the bears. As they drew near the human beings' camp, the wolves heard dogs howling and barking and raising an uproar. There was no reason for the dogs to be raising their voices and waking the whole countryside. The wolves seized the first few dogs that they came upon and dragged them back to the forest. A messenger was at once sent to call the bears to return home for an important meeting.

When all the bears and animals had returned, the wolves dragged the dogs to the centre of the meeting place deep in the forest. They let everyone know that the dogs bayed near the villages of human beings for no good reason except to put the human beings on the alert. And as was to be expected, the human beings got ready to defend themselves.

The animals found it hard to believe that one of their own neighbours would actually go to the enemy and tell them what the animals were up to. After some moments of stunned silence there were mutterings and growls and hisses and howls. "Hang them up! Pluck their eyes out! Break their legs! Drown them! Cut out their tongues!" With each shout there were loud whines of agreement. "Yes! Yes! Yes!"

"No! No! No!" croaked an old raven. "Breaking their legs, plucking their eyes out, yanking their teeth out is too good for them! Wait! I have a better idea. Since they like human beings so much, let the dogs go and live with the two-legged beings and see if the humans like them as much. Let them be as our enemies, no longer welcome in our midst or in our forests or meadows. Let them lick human beings' feet. Let them wag their tails and hunt for them and do everything that their masters bid them do. Let them do what they can to win their masters' affection and love, and see how much good it does them. Instead of thanks, the humans will repay them with kicks, blows with sticks; they will be driven outside to shiver in the rain, snow and cold, and they will be offered meatless bones and scraps of food unfit for human consumption. They will always be hungry for food, and hungry for love. Seldom will they get what they most long for, a pat on the head, a sign of love."

And just as the old raven foretold, so it has been for the dogs.

BEARS — Anishinaubae country was the home of bears, brown and black bears, kin of the Polar and Grizzly Bears. Smaller than their kin, they are nevertheless impressive, commanding respect.

Oral tradition tells us that Kitchi-Manitou entrusted the bears with the duty of keeping Winter Maker from staying too long in Anishinaubae Land, and from being too cold. As a guardian, the bear was a defender, a warrior.

Because of its duties and its unsurpassed care for its offspring, the bear became a totemic symbol for warriors and a model for parenthood.

BEAR MAN

Maudjee-kawiss, Winonah's first born son, came upon a large encampment of Bear people who, it appeared, were holding a great council. He watched them from behind a thicket but he could not hear what they were saying. What fascinated him was the sash that each speaker had draped over one forearm, and pointed to the symbols etched on the vestment as he spoke. Never had he seen or heard such a practice.

In the afternoon the meeting was adjourned. Maudjee-kawiss emerged from his cover and called out and held up his hand to signal that he meant no harm.

The Bear people invited Maudjee-kawiss into their midst. "What are you doing in our part of the country?" they asked him. He explained that he was visiting all the peoples on the Land of the Great Turtle to learn something of their customs, and asked if he might pass through.

After his request was granted, Maudjee-kawiss spoke with his hosts for a while before asking them about the sash that speakers wore over their forearms as they addressed their audience.

"They are wampum sashes (waubumau-peeyauk) that record the deeds, thoughts, dreams, and prayers of our people," the Bear chiefs explained.

Without warning Maudjee-kawiss seized the sash and made off with it, but before he could escape the chief Bear warrior overtook him. Maudjee-kawiss killed him with one blow.

Other warriors were on him the next moment and might have killed Maudjee-kawiss, but the elders intervened. "Don't kill him; such a brave man should be our war chief.... Will you be our war chief?" they asked.

Maudjee-kawiss agreed. But before assuming his duties as chief warrior of the Bear people, Maudjee-kawiss brought the history sash back to his own people so that they too could record their deeds, thoughts, and dreams. Since that time the Anishinaubae people have looked on Bear people as their guardians.

THE BEAR

A certain little boy often went to his grandmother in tears.

"What's wrong?" his grandmother asked.

The little boy whimpered that his parents didn't love him. They whipped him with willow switches; they slapped him; they yelled at him; they told him that he'd never be any good; and he felt like running away from home.

The grandmother spoke to her son and daughter about their son's complaint. "Please show him some kindness. He's just a little child, Kitchi-Manitou's gift to you. Don't abuse him," she said.

The boy's parents promised to take better care of their son and they indeed treated their son with more affection that they had previously shown him. But within months the parents forgot their good intentions; they were as abusive as before.

One evening the boy's parents went about the village angrily looking for their son. They and their neighbours called and called without receiving an answer. The next day and for days after they searched the woods and rivers for the boy. Months later they gave the boy up for dead.

Two years later a party of hunters came upon a bear with her two cubs and a boy. It was the lost boy.

The hunters shouted to get the boy's attention. "Come on home with us. Your parents will be so glad to see you."

"No!" the boy called back. "I want to stay with the bear. She has shown me more kindness than I have ever known. If I go home, I'm afraid that I'll be beaten again for nothing. Tell my parents that I love them."

Bears take better care of their offspring than do some parents.

THE SACRED WHITE BEAR

The Anishinaubae people's first parents were born as twins to Sky Woman. Around her the animals crowded, curious to see what kind of beings the new born infants were. So weak, helpless, pathetic in their cries compared to their own offspring.

When Sky Woman's breasts went dry, the twins cried even more often for food. Sky Woman asked the animals to bring food to keep her children alive.

And they did. They brought honey, seeds, berries, fruit, worms and even flies. But these foods didn't make the twins as strong or as supple as they ought to have been. They remained weak, causing their mother to fret.

What the humans needed, the animals decided, was flesh, meat, something solid. But who was to give his life or hers? They argued. They looked at each other. When it appeared that no one was going to give life for the sake of the twins, a mother bear volunteered to give her life. She felt sorry for Sky Woman and her children.

For her sympathy and sacrifice, the twins, when grown up, chose the bear to be a symbol of guardianship and motherhood.

From the time of her sacrifice the bear has been regarded as someone special, holy, sacred. When hunters have to kill one out of necessity, they place its skull in a tree above the village so that its spirit continues to watch over the people. It is as well a mark of respect.

In the north dwells a sacred white bear who continues to keep watch, bridling Winter-Maker from being too harsh or too severe with Mother Earth, the animals, or with people.

BEAVERS - "Now it's our sister beaver's turn" the bear bellowed. "Quiet! So that we can hear."

Except for the breathing, there wasn't a sound.

The little beaver felt for the lid, found it and pried. The lid was clamped on solid. The little beaver put the container under her left arm to hold it more tightly. With her right hand the beaver pulled. Too hard. The container slipped from her grasp, the cover flipped away.

"What happened?" those standing nearby asked.

"Little grease fingers dropped her container!" the bear grumbled.

In the hush that followed, beaver was heard sobbing. But there were other sounds in addition to Beaver's sobs. They were gurgling, swishing sounds, soft and steady. What they didn't see was Beaver pushing sand and mud and clay to stop her gift from running away.

"What's that?" the bystanders asked.

"It's my gift. I'm sorry" the beaver whimpered "that I dropped it. But I'm holding it back."

"What is it?" the bystanders demanded.

"It's cool. It's soft ... it's water.... You can drink it. You can wash in it. You can live in it," the beaver boasted.

Birds and animals tasted the water. Some birds swam in it, some animals spent a good part of their waking hours playing in it. Fish leaped in, found it to their liking, and chose to live in it.

When the sun shot into the sky and gave light, the birds and the animals saw the beaver still at work, frantically building a dam to hold back the waters to keep them from escaping. He'd already built a small pond.

That beaver's descendants still build dams and ponds to keep the waters in check. Better than their neighbours, they know the needs of Mother Earth to quench her thirst. In making ponds and swamps, beavers also do a good turn for everyone. They build places for frogs, snakes, turtles, fish and insects to live in, and places where birds may nest and geese and ducks may rest in their migrations. Beaver made ponds are lush with plants and flowers that are rich in food and medicine.

Among the things that our ancestors learned from beavers was to mind your own business and do the work that was assigned to you.

PORCUPINES AND OTHERS - By killing Wolf, albeit unintentionally, First Man had alienated the animals and the birds, though he didn't know it. They had taught him how to hunt; now he didn't need them anymore. They couldn't trust First Man.

The animals had done First Man many favours which he could never repay. To some, not many, he returned the favour, not so much to do so in the spirit of giving something for something received, but more to protect the weak from their assailants. First Man had a soft heart for the downtrodden.

It was First Man who gave the Porcupine quills to defend itself. He had, in his wanderings come upon a bear cuffing an object around, as in play. What the bear was playing with, First Man couldn't see, but he could hear it squeal and whimper each time that the bear batted it.

But the little creature, batted out of reach by the bear, clambered up a tree with limbs and branches spiked with sharp thorns. The bear settled down at the bottom of the tree waiting for the roly poly animal to come down.

First Man broke off a branch from the hawthorne tree, whipped the bear and drove it off. Afterward, First Man removed thorns from the tree which he planted on the back of the animal, with the sharpest and greatest number on its tail.

"Now! No one will bother you" First Man assured the animal that he called "Kaug." He also cautioned "Kaug" not to go around looking for someone to whip. Ever since that time the porcupine has gone about his business of trimming trees without fear of being waylaid by bullies, except for the fisher. The fisher is the only animal that will attack a porcupine without receiving a muzzle full of quills, as do rash dogs.

Our ancestors pretty much left porcupines to do what Kitchi-Manitou had created them to do. When they killed a porcupine for its quills to decorate their jackets and dresses, they also ate the meat. Even though the Anishinaubae peoples preferred other animals' meat, porcupine meat, properly prepared, was a delicacy.

The porcupine eventually got a small measure of revenge on the bear. Seems that the fox had hoodwinked the bear into dropping his tail into the water like a fishing line to catch fish. It was then the coldest spell in mid-winter. The water froze around the bear's long tail, holding the bear prisoner. The bear got loose only by tearing free from his bond, but in doing so he left part of his tail in the ice and in the water.

Snorting mad, the bear went on a rampage. He went charging through the forest looking for the fox. When he caught the fox, the bear would tear him into thin strips of meat. The fox was dead meat already in the bear's mind.

But after spending years looking for the fox and chasing him, the bear got it through his thick skull that he would never catch the fox single handed. He needed help.

The only way that the bear could lure the crafty fox within reach was by issuing him a challenge that he couldn't refuse.

Not long afterwards the bear saw the fox, who was out of reach, of course.

"If you're afraid to stand up to me by yourself, why not get some of your friends, if you have any, and I and my friends will have it out fair and square with you out in the open."

The fox agreed, "Good idea."

After they parted the bear recruited the rattler, the lynx and the wolf, who had his own teeth to grind concerning the fox. The fox meanwhile conned the porcupine, the skunk and the wolverine into going with him by telling them that the bear had been spreading rumours about them, and that he was going to whip them publicly.

On the day of the agreed battle, the bear and his friends went to the battlefield early to take up their positions. The bear, as leader, climbed a tall tree to act as a lookout for his companions, who had hidden in various places near the tall tree.

When he saw the fox, his enemy, and his followers, the bear described them as follows: "The one in the lead is dressed in black and white stripes with a soft plume for his bustle; he's small. The second one is built like a roll of fat with bristles, little spears covering his back and bustle. He waddles like a duck and he's puffing from taking a few steps. Behind him is a wolverine picking up rocks every step along the way. He must have a bag that he's filling up. Looks like he doesn't have guts enough for hand-to-hand fighting. And the fox ... bringing up the rear, ready to turn tail and run. What can one expect?"

As their chief described the weapons carried by the advancing enemy, the rattler, the wolf and the lynx backed deeper and further into their blinds.

First to charge was the lynx, closely followed by the wolf. The skunk turned and fired. The porcupine thrashed its tail. The wolverine snapped its jaws and lifted its leg. The fox yelled out, "Come on down you hairy mushroom!"

Howls and yelps filled the air. The stench from skunk gas and wolverine urine choked everyone except the owners. Even the porcupine was reeling from the stench of skunk gas; he staggered to the tree just as the bear was about to step on the ground.

The bear coughed, gagged. He dropped down on top of the porcupine. The bear let out a horrible shriek as a thousand little spears stuck in his rump. He tore from the battlefield into the nearest lake to cool his rump and to beg the crabs and leeches to pull out the spears.

Meanwhile, the porcupine, who'd had the wind knocked out of him, needed several days to recover from the injuries that he'd suffered to his ribs as a result of having a heavyweight bear fall on top of him.

The fox continued on his own way, often looking back to see if the wolf, the only one who had a chance of overtaking him, was on his tail. He had good reason to be wary, even when asleep.

Ever since he had bamboozled wolf into a beating, the fox has had to look frequently behind him. Before that incident, the fox and wolf were companions, sharing the same food in the same den. But the friendship ended, put to an end by the fox's taste for hoodwinking his companions and neighbours.

Friendship turned into enmity over a little white lie. It had been a hard winter, with food scarce. Fox was fortunate enough to come across a man drawing a toboggan full of fish. He helped himself to a trout, which he took home with him.

Fish weren't the regular fare for the friends, but food scarce as it was, left no reason for complaint. It wasn't as good as partridge or rabbit, but it was food that kept them alive.

"Where'd you get the fish?" Wolf asked.

"In the lake. Where'd you think I'd get it?" the fox retorted flippantly.

The Wolf begged the Fox to tell him where he fished so that he too could do his share in providing food for their meals. For the next several days the fox brought fish, and each evening the wolf pleaded with his friend to let him know where he had got his fish. And each time that the wolf asked, he received the same silly answer. But it was only after he had threatened to wring the fox's neck if he didn't answer that the wolf received a satisfactory explanation as to where the fish came from.

"There's a fisherman that passes by such and such place at the same time every evening, pulling a toboggan with fish piled like wood on it. All you need do is to sneak up behind, jump on the load of fish and heave one overboard. Simple as that; the man'll never notice" the fox told the wolf.

But by the time that the Wolf had received his chance to pilfer some meat and contribute to his survival, the man with the toboggan had caught on to the theft of his fish. To prevent the loss of any more fish, the man tied his cargo firmly to his toboggan.

Of course, when the Wolf leaped aboard the toboggan to heave a fish overboard for his own stomach, he found that the fish was not so easy to remove as the fox had said. He grunted and growled in effort. The commotion that the wolf raised attracted the man's attention.

"Soooo! It's you who's been stealing my food!" the man rasped as he raised his club that he carried just for this kind of occasion. The wolf didn't notice that the toboggan had stopped, so intent was he to remove a fish from the stack. And the man struck the wolf again and again, almost beating the life out of him.

"Don't ever steal my food again! Next time, I'll finish you off!" the man warned the moaning wolf.

Some time later the fox came looking for his friend to see why the wolf hadn't returned. Seeing his friend lying in the snow, the fox asked, "What happened?"

"Get out of my sight," the wolf groaned. "You set me up on purpose; you wanted me dead. For that I'll be after your neck and your life when I get better."

From the tone of the wolf's voice the fox knew that the wolf meant it. He trotted off, wondering what the wolf was driving at. The fox would have liked to know why the wolf was blaming him for the beating that he'd received.

Since that time foxes have seldom travelled carefree, as do the skunk and porcupine, but stop frequently to look around and behind them to see if someone is pursuing them.

MOOSE — The moose, deer, caribou and elk are kin, like brothers and sisters. In their spare time they often used to play the "plum stone game." Before they began playing the game, moose, deer, caribou and elk were all prosperous; they had everything they needed.

But some time after they began playing on a regular basis, the elk had lost their homes, their clothes, and were forced to eat the bark off trees. They were the poorest of beings in the forest. Even their skins were cut and bleeding from the lashes that they suffered in running the gauntlet.

From the regularity of their wins, the moose were suspected of cheating or using sorcery. The fact was that the moose were winning, not regularly but all the time.

The elk sent for Nana'b'oozoo to look into what the moose were doing to win all the games. To conduct the investigation without raising suspicion, Nana'b'oozoo joined the Elk Clan as a visiting elk from another part of the country.

He discovered right away that his rival and enemy, The Giant

Lynx, was in the Elk village disguised as an elk, planted there by the Moose to spread bad luck among the elk. The bad luck medicine was contained in the False Elk's medicine bag, which was supposed to be good luck medicine.

Nana'b'oozoo watched a game as a spectator. At the start of the game the Elk players touched the medicine bag for good luck. They still lost, as usual. They were flogged as if they were thieves, and laughed at so that they began to believe that they weren't as good as the Moose.

Later, when he got the chance, Nana'b'oozoo switched the medicine bags. He then took part in the plum stone game. With the bad luck medicine bag as their talisman, the Moose lost everything that they had taken from the Elk.

The Elk recovered their pride while the Moose lost some of their bravado. They couldn't stand losing. They thirsted for revenge.

The Moose issued another challenge. The Elk accepted the Moose challenge to settle which was stronger. The Elk champion, Nana'b'oozoo in disguise, outdid the Moose champion in a test of strength. The Elk thrashed the Moose.

Beaten and bloodied but not out, the Moose would not back down or give in. Even as they were being kicked and whipped as they ran the gauntlet they bellowed, "We'll be back. Then you'll learn who's better."

The Moose, who could stand a lot of punishment, issued yet another challenge, "Bet our champion can stay under water longer than yours."

The Elk accepted.

On the day of the contest the Elk and the Moose gathered on the shores of the lake to watch and to cheer on their champions.

The Elk, Nana'b'oozoo, was given the honour of being first to start the contest. Underwater a turtle accompanied the Elk, giving him air to breathe from within its shell. With such help the Elk easily beat the Moose.

Still the Moose would not admit defeat and yell "Enough!" They came back again and again until Nana'b'oozoo got tired of competing. To get rid of the Moose Nana'b'oozoo banished them to the Northern swamps, there to live and to subsist on sprouts and water plants.

RABBITS — When Winter Maker came down from the North Pole, he blew the leaves off trees, froze the rivers and lakes, chased some birds south, and some animals underground. He came so quickly that the Anishinaubae peoples had no time to put flints away to start their fires with.

Soon the people were shivering. They had no fire. All their meats were frozen. "What will we do?" they asked Nana'b'oozoo.

Nana'b'oozoo called his friends, the rabbits. He told them that his kin, the human beings, were without fire, so that their children were shivering and crying, and had only frozen meat to eat. Winter Maker was the only one who had fire, which he kept burning in his snow house. His two daughters kept and guarded the fire.

"Who's brave enough to steal some fire from Winter Maker?" Nana'b'oozoo asked.

The rabbits looked at each other and shook their heads, their ears flopped down. "Not me! Not me! Not me!" they cried out.

"Isn't anyone brave enough to try to steal even a small coal?" Nana'b'oozoo asked.

The only sound to be heard in the forest was a rattle of rabbits' knees knocking. Finally a little rabbit croaked, "If nobody wants to go, then I'll go, but where is Winter Maker's snow house?"

"I'll take you there," Nana'b'oozoo said. "Come with me." And Nana'b'oozoo led the little rabbit to the shore of a lake. Through the trees, Nana'b'oozoo pointed to a house on the shore opposite. A wisp of smoke curled up from the smoke-hole. "Now, all you have to do is sneak into the house, grab a burning ember, and put it in this little pouch ... and run back here. Don't worry about Winter Maker's daughters. They won't do anything."

The little rabbit now wished that he had not opened his mouth.

He wanted to go home. He was frightened. He crossed the slippery ice.

On the other side of the lake he scrambled over the ice-covered rocks, and in three hops was at the door of Winter Maker's snow-house. The door was locked, but he could hear the voices of girls.

How was he to get inside? His heart thumped, he was so scared. The little rabbit stood there on his hind legs, as if rooted to the spot.

While he stood there near the door, not knowing whether to run or knock, the door opened. The little rabbit was so scared stiff that he couldn't move.

Seeing the little rabbit, the girl crooned, "Aaaah! What a pretty little thing you are, just like a kitten, so cuddly! Come here! Let me pick you up." The little rabbit wanted to bolt for the woods, but his legs wouldn't move. The girl picked the little rabbit up and carried him into the snow-house.

"Look what I found," the girl drooled to her sister. "It's so soft. Aaaah, poor thing. It won't stop shivering, it's so scared." And the little girl held the little rabbit even closer and stroked its fur.

It was warm in the snow-house. The girls were kind, taking turns holding him and giving him meat and fish and dried berries. The food made the little rabbit sick, and the fire frightened him. Flames licked the air, wood sizzled, and sparks leaped out of a yellow-red bed of coals.

Just as the little rabbit was losing some of its fear, Winter Maker came home.

The girls squealed and giggled. "Oh, daddy. Look at what we found."

"Cook it! Boil it! Roast it!" Winter Maker roared.

"No!" the girls cried out. "He's our pet."

Winter Maker snatched the little rabbit out of his daughter's arms, and he pitched the little rabbit into the fire.

"Eeeeeeyooooh!" the little rabbit screamed as he landed in the middle of the blazing logs. His coat caught fire. He screamed again, "Eeeeeeyooooh!" and he bolted out of the lodge. Like a ball of fire, leaving a trail of smoke, the little rabbit raced across the ice. Back home he fled.

As the little rabbit raced ashore on his own side of the lake, Nana'b'oozoo caught him. He wrapped the little rabbit in rolls of birch bark. The bark caught on fire. Last, Nana'b'oozoo put some kindling and wood on the burning birch bark.

While Nana'b'oozoo was building fire, the little rabbit rolled around in the snow to put the fire out. He was singed brown.

Far off in the woods wolves howled, foxes yipped, cougars growled, wolverines snarled. Closer they came, howling for blood.

Nana'b'oozoo called out to them, "Friends! Brothers! Why so angry?"

"A rabbit stole our friend's fire! We're going to kill the rabbits."

"Wait! Can you wait for just a while?" Nana'b'oozoo asked.

Winter Maker's friends stopped in their tracks. They grumbled, "What are we waiting for? Make it snappy!"

Nana'b'oozoo ran into the evergreen forest. He called the rabbits together. "Run! Hide! Stay in the thickets! Watch! Listen!" And by magic, he made all the rabbits as white as snow.

Then he went back to Winter Maker's friends. "I'm all done," he told them.

Off the Winter Maker's friends raced, into the forest to hunt down 'rabbits'.

Soon there were howls. "I can't see a thing! Where have the rabbits gone? The snow's too deep! I can't run!"

Next day Nana'b'oozoo called the rabbits together again. He told them to stay in the evergreen forests, to make trails for their travels, and to come out of their hiding places only at night. In winter, he promised that he would make them white as snow, and in the spring he would change the colour of their coats to brown, a burnt brown, the colour of the rabbit whose coat was singed by fire, as a reminder of their help in getting fire back to the people. The colour, brown, would make it difficult for Winter Maker's friends to see them. "When your coat begins to turn 'brown', you will know that Summer Maker will soon send Winter Maker packing."

The rabbits thanked Nana'b'oozoo.

They made little trails in the densest part of the forest. These little trails led from one shelter to another, from one feeding ground to another, where they fed on willow, maple and other little shoots. They often stopped in their tracks to stand on their hind legs, quivering from the top of their ears to the tips of their toes. The little rabbits were ever ready to run the moment they heard a sound or saw a shadow. Some little rabbits didn't listen. They got careless, even daring owls and wolves to catch them. They didn't get away with their carelessness or their teasing. They were snatched up and carried away. Men and women found the trails and set snares to catch them.

"Why do men and women want to kill us?" the little rabbits asked.

The little rabbits shivered. "Why does everyone pick on us?" they asked. "We're tired of running and hiding, eating the same old food, going to the same places. When is winter going to end?" they asked.

"Soon! Be patient!" the older rabbits answered.

After play one morning, the little rabbits went home to their warrens to rest.

"Look at you! All dirty! Get cleaned up this instant! How did you get your coats so dirty?" the mothers scolded.

The little rabbits looked at each other. Their coats were soiled, tinged with brown.

"But mom! We were just playing in the snow!" and the little rabbits looked at their mothers. They asked their mothers how they had gotten their own coats dirty.

The mother rabbits looked at their coats. It was true. Their coats were dabbed with a touch of brown.

An old grandmother rabbit, Mother Bun they called her, reminded them. "Do you remember what Nana'b'oozoo said about our coats changing colour?"

"Yes! ... Yes!"

"And that spring would not be long in coming?"

"Yes! ... Yes!"

The little rabbits jumped up and down. They sang and cheered. Then they danced round and round, here and there. The rabbits held a Spring Pow-wow. They left their tracks all over.

Hunters, wolves, foxes, cougars who came to hunt them didn't know where to start, which trail to follow. There were so many rabbit tracks in the snow. The rabbit hunters gave up. They went home.

Every year, in late winter, the rabbits put on brown coats, and when they feel the warm breath of Summer Maker, they dance and dance, every night until the snow is all gone. They have a Spring Pow-wow.

FISH

Our ancestors are more often depicted as hunters than they are as fishers. Perhaps this is because hunting is more demanding and more rewarding than is fishing in that the quarry yields not only meat but clothing, tools and lessons in life.

But fishing may not have been secondary to hunting as a way of stocking the food racks and filling pots and bowls with food. Fish, easier to catch than animals, were as much a staple as were deer, moose, beaver and other animals.

Until recent times there were so many fish that the waters were said to be alive with fish. The storytellers may not have been exaggerating when they said that when a school of fish passed in the shallows or over a shoal, the bottom of the lake could not be seen. No one, not otters, hawks, kingfishers, seagulls, ducks, or herons, needed to stretch a muscle to fill their stomachs. It was as easy for humans to put a meal in their pots. Go down to the riverbank and spear a fish. There was no need to fret about the next meal. It was there for the taking in the wellspring of the lake.

The waters of lakes, rivers and seas were generous, abundant beyond saying. It was like the soul-spirit of man, shrouded in mystery. What lurked in the depths, out in the middle of the sea, no one could say. Beyond a few feet no one could see the bottom, no matter how bright the sun. Only the fish and the turtles knew, but they kept what they knew secret.

Men and women guessed what, besides fish and turtles, dwelt in the bottom of the seas and lakes. They were sure that there were mermen and mermaids, sea serpents, Giant Lynx's, Giant Sturgeon, Giant Trout, Giant Turtles, and unfriendly manitous. Water was their world.

Possessive and jealous, they were unwilling to admit anyone to visit their world or to pass over from one shore to another without asking for permission and offering tobacco. Fish were alien, living in an alien world.

The waters in which fish dwelt gave humans life, others it pulled down into its murk where it transformed them into fish.

Our ancestors thought of the seas, rivers and lakes as fountain-heads and as the Underworld, inhabited by Giant Fish and Giant Animals set on the destruction of humans and animals who dared trespass upon their world.

The enmity between land beings and water beings began soon after human beings were created. It was supposed to have started in the following manner.

Meegis Meegwun (Shell Feather) had bullied a certain community for as long as anyone could remember. The people weren't strong enough to defeat Meegis Meegwun, and when they resisted, the warrior took their children and kept them captive in his island stronghold which was guarded by fire breathing sea serpents.

On learning that there was a certain half manitou, half man by the name of Nana'b'oozoo who championed the weak, the people invited him to rid them of their oppressor. To get at Meegis Meegwun, Nana'b'oozoo killed the sea serpents that guarded the island home of the enemy. In killing the sea serpents, Nana'b'oozoo incurred the hatred of other serpents and monsters that were kin of the victims.

One in particular, more dangerous than the rest, occupied Kitchi-Gummeeng, Lake Superior. It was he who caused the storms in the fall when he went hunting for food. During these days fishers kept near shore. Even when it was calm it was not safe to go too far out from land. The monster could stir up a storm at any time.

In one village the monster, the Giant Sturgeon, had come right to the shores to seize some children who were then playing at the water's edge.

Nana'b'oozoo felt sorry for his kinsmen. He'd settle scores with the monster on the people's behalf.

Aboard a raft that he'd constructed, Nana'b'oozoo went out to the middle of the sea to fish. As he cast his line, Nana'b'oozoo had his singing sticks, and chanted:

Where is that overgrown minnow
That feeds on minnows?
Come! Feed on me
If you dare
If you can stir from your bed.

When the lure struck the face of the Giant Sturgeon, the great fish sent the whitefish to return the lure back to the fisher. Nana'b'oozoo tossed the whitefish back into the sea, telling it that "Nana'b'oozoo wants a fish to boil, not a minnow."

Nana'b'oozoo cast his line into the sea a second time. Again he chanted:

Is there a fish in the sea?
Or are there only minnows?
Must I starve

While you grow fat

And cannot stir from your bed.

Though he was provoked by the lure that dangled in front of his face, the Giant Sturgeon still would not leave its bed. He sent a trout to take the lure back to its owner.

"Tell that overgrown minnow that I would dry its flesh upon the rocks and feed it to the fish hawks ... if the fish hawks will eat it," Nana'b'oozoo told the trout as he pitched it back into the sea.

Nana'b'oozoo lowered his line a third time. He chanted:

All weight

All fat you must be.

If you had heart

You'd rise from your torpor

To take my bait.

Stung by the words, the Giant Sturgeon rose from its bed and broke surface with a thunderous roar and, as it did so, swallowed Nana'b'oozoo and his raft in one mighty gulp.

In the Giant Sturgeon's belly Nana'b'oozoo could neither see nor hear, he could only sense motion and dread. Eventually Nana'b'oozoo's heart beat settled down.

"Nana'b'oozoo!" someone called in the dark. "Light a torch."

Nana'b'oozoo fumbled around in the dark in his travel bag until he found his flints and tinder. Not having a proper dried branch, Nana'b'oozoo used one of his arrows as a torch.

In the dim light Nana'b'oozoo saw the bones of many animals that the Giant Sturgeon had eaten, and the children that the monster had swallowed.

"Nana'b'oozoo!" the same little voice that had spoken to him earlier called out. "If you have a knife, strike here. Keep stabbing. Don't stop."

"But I don't want to hurt him," Nana'b'oozoo argued. "It will only get him madder. Better that we dance and dance until he gets sea sick and throws us up on land."

"That will only make him madder," the little voice of a little squirrel explained. "He'll get back at us even more. Better to finish him."

When Nana'b'oozoo saw the sense in the squirrel's explanation, he set to work. He struck again and again until his arm hurt and he had to sit down to rest. While Nana'b'oozoo was resting there was drumming and chanting somewhere above them. Nana'b'oozoo cringed, and asked the squirrel what the drumming meant.

"It means" the squirrel told him, "that the seagulls and herons, fish hawks and turtles are already dismembering the Giant Sturgeon."

When those who were swallowed by the Giant Sturgeon were all free on land, they all celebrated a festival.

After the festival, Nana'b'oozoo cut up the Giant Sturgeon and threw the pieces into the sea. As he flung the pieces into the waters, Nana'b'oozoo put a curse on each one, saying, "You'll never eat humans again; humans and birds will now eat you. You'll never again be giant in size, but you will be numerous and ... different. You will be trout, suckers, whitefish, pike, pickerel, bass, perch, sunfish, herring, rock bass, small sturgeon."

The fish dove into the sea out of sight and multiplied. Instead of human and animal flesh, the fish fed on water bugs, insects, water mosses, water plants and kept the sea and the bottom of sea clean.

The sea was good. The sea was generous. Its yield was boundless.

Patience was all that was needed to catch fish. Few were better than the herons, ospreys, and kingfishers at catching fish. All that the heron did was to stand in the water for a little while and wait for a fish to come to its side. It was as simple as that.

Once Nana'b'oozoo learned patience, he got all the fish that he wanted. He'd never go hungry. Fishing provided sure meals.

Yet Nana'b'oozoo wasn't satisfied. Going out every day to catch one fish for one meal was a waste of time. Far better for a person to catch a pile of fish, smoke and dry them and store them away. Then there'd be no need to go to work for months.

Inspired by this marvellous idea, Nana'b'oozoo set to work, extra hours, overtime, double-time, and in a few days had caught a stack of fish. Tired and hugely pleased, Nana'b'oozoo fell asleep, leaving his grandmother alone to gullet and filet the fish for drying and smoking.

While Nana'b'oozoo slept and his grandmother was busy, crows, ravens, buzzards, hawks, mice, raccoons and other pirates came along and helped themselves to the free food. Awakened by his grandmother to the open theft of their provisions by the freeloaders, Nana'b'oozoo spent the next while beating off the raiders. It was useless. Nana'b'oozoo created more work for himself and for his grandmother in order to save himself work.

Nana'b'oozoo's experience didn't serve as much of a lesson for some people.

In more recent times Bondy, a fisherman from Wikwemikong, Ontario, received a chilling warning from the bay to keep his greed in check.

His fellow fishermen described him as greedy. First one out on the lake in the morning, took the shortest lunches, and always had to make one more round trip before turning in to land.

Yet his fellow fishermen continued to invite him to go ashore with, "Time for lunch!" and sometimes, "Time for one more round trip."

But one time he made one more round trip and then no more. When Bondy came ashore, instead of unpacking his lunch and making tea, he just sat down on a log as if he were sick.

At first nobody said anything to him. Then when Bondy hadn't stirred, his friends asked him what was wrong. He answered, "nothing" but the other fishermen knew that something was wrong. They could tell from the complexion of his skin, from the dilation of his eyes. His "nothing" meant "I don't want to talk about it" and the men left him alone.

Except for one, Trudeau. He remained by Bondy's side. He wouldn't leave Bondy alone. "There's something wrong, I can tell. I know. Tell me."

Finally Bondy relented. "I s'saw ... a s'sea-serpent, near the boat ... a head like a horse's with humps on his back." Bondy slurred and stammered as if he still saw the monster.

"I'll get you some tea," Trudeau promised the man.

At their campfire Trudeau told his companions that Bondy had seen 'a sea serpent.' Some moments passed by without a word before one of the other fishermen quipped, "He should have clubbed it. I heard that they are good to eat."

At any other time the other men would have roared, but this time they bit their tongues to keep from laughing aloud. Later, they'd laugh.

Bondy went home that afternoon. Never went fishing again. Sold his boat and his equipment. As much as people believed that Nana'b'oozoo had slain all the sea monsters, they are still there in rivers, lakes, bays.

SPIRIT SOUL TROUT

Tell me, friend
You who dwells in the dark and deep
How I may venture unafraid
Into the dark world of half death.

I give You thanks, Great Spirit, from the bottom of my heart
For granting my humble petition
To live yet another day, and
To see and draw strength and nourishment
For body and soul from the Earth,
Mother of all that we are
Anishinaubaek, other First Nations, other races, and
The eagle, the bear, the whitefish, the butterfly
And all their kin.

I give You thanks, Great Spirit,
For having shown Your compassion

My wife
Our children
Our grandchildren
Our friends and
Our neighbours

Look with favour upon our prayers.
Watch over us and bear us safely through the darkness
To re-awaken at dawn
One in family and one in community.

SOUL TROUT
My friend
When my spirit at dawn
Reunites with its soul and flesh
I awaken and thank our Maker

I give you thanks, Great Spirit
For having compassion upon me, and
Granted my petition
To keep and safeguard my body and soul, this night past
So that I may remain in the company of my loved ones.
My wife
Our children
Our grandchildren
Our friends, and
Our neighbours
And live yet another day to reap the benefits of your bounty
As I pass another milestone along this Path of Life.
I pray as well
That You may bestow as much compassion and benevolence
Upon our people, as You have done me, and
Grant their petitions, fulfillment.

FISH
After killing a deer, grouse or fish
The native people thanked the Creator for
The bounty of the earth and the sea.
They gave thanksgiving as well
To their victim.

Meegawaetchiwi-audauh gayae
K'bim-gaedauguninaunik
Waesseehnuk, benaessiwuk, geegoohnuk gayae
W'gee pagidinumaukooying w'bim-audiziwiniwauh
Tchi ishko-nae-ing keeyaubih ningo-geezhig.

Let us give thanksgiving
To our co-tenants upon this earth
The deer, the geese, the fish
Who gave their lives so that
We might live to see another day.

THOU SHALT HONOUR EARTH MOTHER

Long before the Anishinaubaek or other people were set upon the earth, and continuing to this day, birds, animals, insects and fish were abiding by certain principles.

Robins, as did their kin and kind, came and went as they pleased; they left their perches and returned when they pleased. No master commanded them where, when or how to build their nesting places. It was they, and no other, who decided where, when and how to carry out what Kitchi-Manitou had intended them to do. Robins are free, as are other creatures.

And who among the ravens, buffalo, ants contributed more to the earth, to their kin and neighbours, to creation? Who among the ravens is the blackest, swiftest, keenest of eye? Who among the buffalo scores and scars the earth more deeply? Whose hooves thunder more loudly than any other? Who among the ants carries the heavier burden? Or draws more sweat? Whose passing draws more tears? Do such questions arise among them? Do they fight about these matters? Does one life mean more than any other to Kitchi-Manitou? Does Kitchi-Manitou give more to some? Less to others? No! No one is more important than any other. They are all born equal, all have some purpose in furthering creation, Kitchi-Manitou's work.

There is not a bird, animal, insect, fish that is without a place where, with a mate, it will create new life and where it will serve its own needs in its own way, and where it will nourish its soul and spirit. Hawks build their nests in trees, badgers dens within the earth, and spiders their webs in dark recesses. The homes that hawks, badgers and spiders make for themselves belong to them and to their offspring, and so long as they need to dwell in one place and draw what they need to eat from the neighbourhood so long may they drive off intruders and trespassers from their homes.

Beating back invaders and raiders is the way that hawks, badgers and spiders proclaim ownership of their homes. "This is my home! Kitchi-Manitou has granted me this place as my home. I mean to keep what the Creator has given to me."

All creatures, great and small, whether they be bears or bees, have the sense of ownership.

Every spring, even before the snow has melted, birds begin their return from their winter sanctuary somewhere in the south. They are filled with song and chant, warble and whistle from sunrise to sunset. They chant through snow, rain and cold winds. And for what purpose do they chant? They chant to proclaim their joy and thanksgiving to Kitchi-Manitou, to Mother Earth and to each other. Robins, bluebirds, sparrows are grateful for life, beauty, health, food, music, home, offspring. Each one thanks Kitchi-Manitou and Mother Earth in his own way, with his own song.

To our ancestors it was self evident that all creatures were born equal and free to come and go and fulfill their purposes as intended by Kitchi-Manitou. All were entitled to a place on this earth where they might raise their offspring and offer their thanksgiving to the Creator.

Kitchi-Manitou has done no less for men and women. The Creator has made us equal, given us freedom to come and to go, a place to grow in spirit and nurture our dreams, and leave to talk to the manitous in our own way whenever it was meant to do so.

And so the Anishinaubaek came and went as they pleased, without having to ask permission of the chief or some master.

Men and women stood, sat, talked, walked, and worked with chiefs and leaders. They were equal.

Men and women had homes, for to have them was an inborn need. They needed a place unto themselves and their mates where they could create new life and being, nurture the gifts that Kitchi-Manitou had bestowed upon them, and where they could be themselves and reflect upon the progress that they had made in their passage along the Path of Life and dwell upon the fulfillment of their dreams and duties.

For Anishinaubae men and women, home was and is "aeindauyaun," a place that belongs to me and where I long to be. It's a place where I can be myself and not disturb my neighbours. The term "indauwin" comes from the same root as does "indiwin" which means culpability, accountability, mood, disposition. The good or evil that men and women did was understood to have been bred and nurtured in the home; and credit or blame assigned as deserved.

The owners of dwellings had no need to proclaim to their neighbours or the world that the wigwaum they occupied and the land that their home was settled on belonged to them and to no other. Kitchi-Manitou endowed this sense of ownership into the hearts of all men and women. Only Kitchi-Manitou can endow such a sense in human beings; only Kitchi-Manitou can take back this sense, but doesn't.

Our ancestors had everything to be thankful for: the land that

Kitchi-Manitou had given them was beautiful and fertile. Its mountains glistened with snow; its valleys were lush with orchards; its forests echoed with the calls of birds and animals; rivers and lakes flashed silver with the forms of fish; its meadows were o'erspread with flowers. The land yielded harvests more than enough to feed all living creatures.

The land gave forth food in abundance; it also unfolded whatever men and women needed to understand to know about life and being. Every day, every season, every year something takes place that reflects some aspect of our world, our existence, our conduct, and our destiny. There is birth, growth, maturation, degeneration, death, regeneration and transformation. What a man or a woman gleans that adds to his or her understanding is revelation. The earth holds nothing back from those who open up their senses (except the next life).

Some glean more from their observations, others less, but each one in proportion to his talents. What one person understands of what he sees or hears is not to be belittled, demeaned, or ridiculed. For how is anyone to know for certain that he is right and another, wrong? And if such a person were to say that another is wrong, it would be arrogant. Where differences in opinion occurred, men and women said Kitchi-Manitou has given me a different understanding.

By sharing their observations our ancestors increased and spread their knowledge. Storytellers would spin stories about creation, where the living came from, where the dead went; they told stories about the Path of Life and how to remain on the right trail, and warned listeners what it was that caused people to lose their way and what they were to do to get back on the right trail.

What our ancestors found about the world was sacred; everything was sacred by virtue of its creation by Kitchi-Manitou, and everything was sacred because every form of life had an element of mystery. A deer, buffalo, bear, partridge have something called chechauk (soul) that holds flesh and spirit together. A tree, a blade of grass, a seed has this element. It is the breath of life that Kitchi-Manitou has given to every being. It belongs to the creature receiving it and to Kitchi-Manitou who granted it. When a hunter needed to kill an animal or a bird or a fish for his family, he asked Kitchi-Manitou to grant him permission to take the life of his intended victim. On killing his quarry the hunter offered tobacco in thanksgiving to Kitchi-Manitou and words of regret to his victim. Life is sacred.

Our ancestors talked and chanted to Kitchi-Manitou, to the grandfathers and grandmothers, to the spirits of the birds, animals, insects and fish to thank them for benefits received or to beseech Kitchi-Manitou to help them control selfishness, fear, jealousy, vengeance, pride and other shortcomings, and to grant them instead selflessness, courage, health, goodwill, good dreams, kindness, humour, a forgiving spirit and wisdom.

Men and women talked to Kitchi-Manitou, Earth Mother (Mizzu-kummik-quae) and other manitous, alone, using their own words. Men and women talked to the Creator, Earth Mother, wherever and whenever they felt the need to say something or to ask for some favour. They didn't need a holy person to guide them, nor did they recite prayers from memory. No; they spoke freely from their hearts.

They talked to Earth Mother as they would another person, as if the earth could hear and understand and talk back. They told her that she was beautiful, and thanked her for her bounty. Each spring they asked her to be as bounteous as in the past, and beseeched the Thunderbirds to keep Earth Mother fresh and fertile. That every being was indebted to Earth Mother was in their minds.

The pipe of peace ceremony exemplifies the regard that our ancestors had for Earth Mother. In the ceremony the celebrant offered the first whiff of tobacco smoke to Kitchi-Manitou and the next to Earth Mother. The offerings of smoke were expressions of honour, respect, love, gratitude. If the pipe smoking ceremony were a series of acts depicting commandments, the second whiff to the Earth would decree "Thou shalt honour Earth Mother."

GLOSSARY

Agaum: **The other shore of an island, continent**
Ani-geeshk-aubikauh: **A scarp, an escarpment**
Aunikae-ginoo-aeyaung: **An isthmus (also ginoon-aeyaung)**
Auyauniko-dunnauh: **A mountain range**

Beetoo-ipeeg(oon): **A pond(s)**

Gummee, gummeen: **A large body of water, sea, ocean**
Gaug-eedjiwun(oon): **A falls, cascade(s)**
Geeshk-aubikauh-dunnauh: **A gorge**

Ishkotae-dunnauh: **A volcano**
Ishp-aubikauh-dunnauh: **A mountain range**

Kaka-dunnauh: **A mountain chain**
Kaukauh-ipeekauh: **A water falls, cascade**
Kitchi-gaum: **A continent**
Kitchi-gummeeng: **A sea, an ocean**

Maewishkodae(n): **A prairie(s)**
Maumeeng: **Downstream**
Metigwauk-aki(akeen): **A forest(s), woods**
Miniss(un): **An island(s)**
Minitik(oowun) kemauh ministik(oowun): **An island(s) in or at the mouth of a river, formed by silt**
Misheen-maukinaukoong: **North America, Michillimackinac**
Mishi-gummeeng: **Lake Michigan**
Mushkeeg(oon): **A swamp(s), marsh(es)**

Naeyaush: **A point, peninsula**
Nopimeeng: **Inland**

Papiko-dunnauh: **Alpine**
Pushkawauk-dauwingauh: **A desert**
Pussaun-kaun(un): **A ditch, moat, canal**
Tibaewih: **On the shore**
Tikip(een): **A spring(s)**

Waush(un) kemauh waudji(un): **A den(s), cave(s)**
Weemb-aubikauh: **A cave, cavern**
Weequaed(oon): **A bay(s)**
Widjiw(inun): **A mountain(s)**
Zaugeeng: **A river mouth**
Zeepi(een): **A river(s)**
Zaugigun(un) kemauh zaugau-igun(un): **A lake(s)**

SOME WEATHER CONDITION TERMS

Aen-geezhiguk: **The sort of day**
Ae-inaumidaek: **The barometric pressure**
Ae-inauniquok: **The cloud formation**
Anim-akeekauh: **It is thundering**
Aubowaumigut; aubowauh: **It is mild, loosening up**
Cheecheeng-kummikauh: **An earthquake**
Dagoon-ipeessauh: **A rainbow**
Ningawaugun: **A rainbow**
Pishibaubeewoh: **Swirling drifting snow**
Pishibaubee-aunimut: **A whirlwind**
Pishibau-ipeessid-ossaemigut (or just ossae): **A tornado**
Tootoo-kummikauh: **A tremor**
Titibau-ipeessauh: **A tornado, water-spout**
Awun-ipeessauh: **A drizzle attended by mist**
Titabee-aunimut: **A whirlwind**

TREES — METIG(OOK)

Akauwauhnsh(eek): **A juniper(s)**

Baupauss-pigiw-inauk(ook): **A balsam(s)**

Gawaunduk(ook): **A spruce(s)**

Geezhig(ook): **A cedar(s)**

Inin-aunduk(ook): **A spruce(s)**

Inin-autik(ook): **A maple(s)**

Kaugaug-maewish(eek): **A hemlock(s)**

Kaugaug-meesh(eek): **A hemlock(s)**

Kaugaug-meen-gauwuhnsh(eek): **A sumac(s)**

Mamaundau-metig(ook): **A lilac(s)**

Meenaus-gauwuhnsh(eek): **A hawthorn(s)**

Metig-maewish(eek): **A red oak(s)**

Metig-waubauk(ook): **A hickory(ies)**

Mishee-meeni-gauwuhnsh(eek): **An apple tree(s)**

Mishi-maewish(eek): **A white oak(s)**

Misqwauwauk(ook): **A red cedar(s)**

Mooninoohnse(uk): **An ironwood**

Mushkeeg-wautik(ook): **A tamarack(s)**

Neep(eek, ikook): **An elm(s)**

Niteemish(uk): **An ash (white)**

Okikaehnse(uk): **Jack pine(s)**

Paukawangaemauk(ook): **Pine(s) - red**

Peepeegwunaushk(ook): **An elder(s)**

Waedoop-(ikook): **An alder(s)**

Weegoop(eek): **A basswood(s)**

Weegwauss(uk): **A birch(es)**

Weenisk (weenisik) ook: **A birch(es) - yellow**

Weessigauk(ook): **An ash - black**

Zaudee(k): **Poplar(s)**

Zeezigoob-maewish(eek): **A willow(s)**

Zhawaemish(eek): **A beech(es)**

Zheeg-maewish(eek): **A maple(s) - soft**

Zhingob(eek): **A fern(s)**

Zhingwauk(ook): **A pine(s)**

PLANTS — FLOWERS

Agidae-bug(oon): **Marsh marigold(s)**

Anauk(oon): **A bullrush(es)**

Aundaeg-bugoohnse(un): **Wild mint**

Aneeb-meen-gauwuhnsh: **High bush cranberries**

Anim-akeebug(oon): **Poison ivy**

Anung-piko-ipeessae-bug(oon): **Water lily(ies) - white**

Gauwaug-bugoohnse(uk): **A rose(s)**

Gauzhug-aehnsewi-bug(oon): **Catnip**

Gazheeb-dayae-meeni-gauwuhnsh: **Hawthorn bush(es)**

Geezisso-mashki-aki: **Goldenrod**

Gunkissaehn-meeni-bug(oon): **Lily of the Valley**

Ishkotae-bugoonee(n): **Cardinal flower**

Kaudauk(oon): **Queen Anne's lace**

Kundoomoon(un): **Water lily - yellow**

Maewishk, maewishkoon: **Hay**

Meewishk, meewishkoon: **Hay**

Maewishush-maewishkoon: **Hay**

Matchi-manitou-saemauh: **Mullein**

Matchi-mashki-abi-meen: **Nightshade**

Meen-bug-auwuhnsh(eek): **Blueberry plant(s)**

Mindemoyaehn(uk): **Dandelion(s)**

Misqui-cheebik(oon): **Bloodroot**

Mizaunushk: **Thistle**

Muk-akee-bug: **Jewel weed**

Mushkeeg-bugoohnse: **A small tamarack**

Mushkeeg-meen-gauwuhnsh(eek): **Cranberry bush(es)**

Nae-nissowae-buguk: **Clover - red**

Nana'b'oozoo okomissun meenississun: **Indian paint brush**

Nana'b'oozoo pigook: **Canada lily**

Naunaugunushk(oon): **Ferns**

Nomino-ginae-guhnshk(oon): **St. John's wort**

Nubug-ushk(oon): **Sweetflag**

Numae-pin: **Wild ginger**

Onaunigizidaun-bug(oon): **Plantain**

Pukawaeyauk-igin(een): **Cat-tail**

Saemauhnushk: **Tobacco**

Tootaugauhnse: **Harebell**

Wae-wauwiyaeyau-bugug: **Violet**

Wau-babau-bego-dayaeshing(ik): **Day lily(ies)**

Weekaehn: **Sweetflag**

Weekizigun: **Doll's eyes**

Weengushk: **Sweet grass**

Wee-nissi-meen also (bug): **Wintergreen**

Weessauk-cheechauk-meen-bug: **A rose bush**

Weessugi-bug: **Burdock**

Zauwunushk(oon): **Mustard**

Zeend-augun: **A sunflower**

Zhaushaug-meen: **Bunchberry(ies)**

Zhaubo-meen-ushk(oon): **Gooseberry(ies)**

VEGETABLE(S) — MEEDJIM

Cheesi(un): **Turnip(s)**

Choogin(eek): **Tomato(es)**

Koossimaun(un): **Pumpkin(s)**

Maundau-meen(uk): **Corn**

Mino-meen: **The so-called "Wild Rice"**

Mitchig-meen(uk): **Cucumber(s)**

Pin(eek): **A potato(es)**

Waubauk-idaeyauh: **A parsnip(s)**

Wauweewi-quae-idjeeyauh: **A cabbage(s)**

Zauwaukoot(oon): **A carrot**

Zhigaug-wuhnsh(eek): **An onion(s)**

INSECTS, WORMS, MITES — MANITOUSHUK

Abidushkoon-aesheehn(uk): **A dragonfly (flies)**

Aehnsi-gauk(ook): **A wood louse (lice), a tick(s)**

Aenig(ook): **An ant(s)**

Aeyaebig(ook): **A spider(s)**

Aumoohn(uk): **A bee(s); (the repeller)**

Cheecheegau-waessih(wuk): **A beetle(s)**

Koodjeesh(uk): **A louse (lice)**

Kookoowaessih(wuk): **A moth(s)**

Mae-minau-auwidjissaehn(uk): **A cricket(s)**

Maemaegawaehnshish(uk): **A caterpillar(s)**

Maemaegawauhnse(wuk): **A butterfly(flies); (a little feather)**

Mishi-aumoohn(uk): **A bumblebee(s)**

Mizizauk(ook): **A horsefly(flies)**

Niminau-goodjissaehn(uk): **A water-spider(s)**

Noonimoodoo-waessih(wuk): **A chrysalis**

Odjee(k): **A common housefly(ies)**

Ooquae(k): **A maggot**

Pigook-issaehnse(wuk): **A blackfly(flies)**

Pinee-manitoush(wuk): **A potato bug(s)**

Pingwoosh(uk): **A sandfly(flies)**

Pubig(ook): **A flea(s)**

Pukinae(k): **A grasshopper**

Skinauk(ook): **A nit(s)**

Supkaesheehn(k): **A spider(s); netmaker(s)**

Tibauk-waugunaenikaesseehn(uk): **A caterpillar(s)**

Tissau-waesheehn(uk): **A cicada(s)**

Wauwautaessih(wuk): **A firefly(flies)**

Zhiginauhn(uk): **An earthworm(s)**

Zigimaehn(uk): **A mosquito(es); (to cling to)**

SOME COMMON BIRDS

Aundaeg(ook): A crow(s) (where?)

Baeshkeewae(k): A nighthawk; meaning one who is hoarse

Benae(wuk): A partridge(s)

Cheecheesh-kawaehn: A killdeer(s), plover(s); meaning one that leaves trailing footprints

Cheecheeb-quaewaessih(wuk): A killdeer(s); meaning one whose head bobs back and forth

Chechauk(ook): A crane(s); meaning soul(?)

Deendeehnse(wuk): A bluejay(s)

Geekabeek-maesheehn(k): A meadowlark(s)

Geeshk-munisseehn(k): A kingfisher; meaning one who produces a ripping sound

Kaikaik(ook): A hawk(s)

Kaugaugeehn(k): A raven(s), the ever-present bird

Kaugauk-isheehn(k): A raven(s), the ever-present bird

Kauyaushk(ook): A seagull(s)

Kineu(wuk): The bald headed eagle(s)

Kookookoo(k): Owl(s). The Great Horned Owl

Maemae(k): The flicker(s)

Maung(ook): A loon(s)

Meemee(k): A dove(s), pigeon(s)

Migizi(wuk): Golden or Brown Eagle

Mino-meenikaesheehn(k): A snipe(s) that habituates wild rice

Mooning-wunaehn(k): A crested plover

Nau-noogishk-auhnse(iwuk): A hummingbird; one that steps here and there

N'sheemaehn(k): A chickadee(s); my younger brother(s) or sister(s)

Naubae-ossae(wuk): A rooster, one that struts about like a male

Nikah, nikuk: A goose, geese

Paupaussae(k): A woodpecker(s); a knocker

Pitchi(wuk): A robin(s), an accident or during

Pukwaun-audjeehn(k): A bat(s), one that frequents roof(s)

Siginauk(ook): **A blackbird(s)**

Waewae(k): **Canada Goose (geese)**

Waub-anung-issaehn(k): **A snowbird(d); white stars in motion**

Waubizee(k): **A swan(s). To be the image of white**

Weenaungaehn(k): **A buzzard(s); at home in dirt and uncleanliness**

Weendigo-benaessih(wuk): **A king bird(s); a cannibal bird**

Zauwae-benaessih(wuk): **A canary(ies); a yellow bird**

Zhaedae(k): **A pelican(s)**

Zhaushauwi-benaessih(wuk): **A swallow(s)**

Zhauwun-aessih(wuk): **A bluebird(s)**

Zheesheeb(uk): **A duck(s)**

Zhooshigauh: **A heron(s); from zhooshi-gauboowih — to stand out**

ANIMALS

Addik(ook; oowuk): **Caribou(s)**

Adjidumooh kemauh odjidumooh: **A squirrel(s); upside down**

Aehnse-bun(uk): **A raccoon(s); formerly a shell**

Amik(ook; oowuk): **A beaver(s); one that dwells at the bottom of a pond**

Bizheu(wuk): **A lynx(es)**

Gageeb-eengawae-quae(wuk): **A mole(s); a blind woman**

Gaween-gauwigaehn(uk): **A wolverine(s)**

Gaween-waeyaugae(uk): **A wolverine(s); uncertain as to which way to go**

Gunkissaehnse(uk): **A chipmunk(s)**

Kaug(ook; oowuk): **A porcupine(s)**

Kitugaukoohnse(uk): **A fawn(s); mottled, speckled**

Kookidjeesh(uk, iwuk): **A groundhog(s), a weaver**

Maemae-quaedoohn(uk): **A mole(s); one that emerges here and there, now and then**

Mishaewae(k) (also Mooshaewae): **An elk(s)**

Mishauk-waukidjeesh(uk, iwuk): **A badger(s)**

Moozoo(k): **A moose; one that trims, shears, clips, cuts the pond and muskeg grasses**

Mukwoh(k, wuk): **A bear(s), a searcher-finder, seeker**

Myeengun(uk): **A wolf, wolves; not trusting, make strange**
Naepaudji-anik-aessih(wuk): **A mole(s); gauche**
Ningik(ook): **An otter(s)**
Odjeek(ook, oowuk): **A fisher(s)**
Pushkawau-dausheehn(k): **A coyote(s), an habitue of open spaces**
Sunigoo(k): **A black squirrel(s)**
Waub-oozoohn(k): **A rabbit(s) — white-tailed**
Waub-ozhaesh(uk, iwuk): **A marten(s); white bodied**
Waugoosh(uk): **A fox(es); the crooked, curved one**
Wauwau-begoonoodjeehn(uk): **A mouse (mice); one that bores here and there**
Wauwaushkaeshih(wuk): **A deer; curved horns**
Wuzhushk(ook): **A muskrat(s); covered with mud**
Zhaungawaeshih(wuk): **A mink(s)**
Zhigaug(ook): **A skunk(s), the urinator, the pisser**
Zhigushk-aundawae(k): **A flying squirrel(s)**
Zhingoohnse(uk): **A weasel(s); a nuisance, pest, annoyance**

SOME COMMON FISH

Addik-maeg(ook): Whitefish, caribou of the waters
Anumae(k): Sturgeon(s), a denizen(s) of the depths
Ashigun(uk): A bass
Gino-ozhae(k): A pike(s), long-bodied
Kaewiss(uk): A herring(s)
Kitchi-maun-maeg(ook): A whale(s)
Maun-maegooss(uk): A catfish, an ugly fish
Mauzh-maegooss(uk): A speckled trout, homely
Zauwi-maegoos(uk): A speckled trout, copper or brown
Mish(k)-gino-ozhae(k): A muskellunge; the great long bodied one
Mizyh(uk): A catfish
Numaebin(uk): A sucker(s), a bottom dweller, feeder
Numaegooss(uk): A trout(s), a deeper water dweller
Ogauh(k): A pickerel(s)

Sauwae(k): Perch(es)

Waussee(k): A sunfish(es), bright shiny

SOME PLACE NAMES

THE GREAT LAKES

Kitchi-Gummeeng or Kitchi-Ojibway Gummeeng: Lake Superior

Mishi-Gummeeng: Lake Michigan, The Great Sea

Odauwau-Gummeeng: Lake Huron, The Sea of the Ottawas

Waussau-Gummeeng: Georgian Bay, The Shining Sea

Kitchi-Waubishkkagow-Gummeeng: Lake Erie, The Great Sea of white breakers

SMALLER LAKES: Zaugau-igunun

Neepeessing: Lake Nipissing

Teemau-gummeeng: Lake Temagami, The deep lake

Wauwiyautinoong: Lake St. Clair, The round, oval place

Ween-ipeeg-isheeng: Lake Winnipeg, The dirty waters

Anim-ipeeg-oong: Lake Nipigon, Along the water's edge: pipe stove lake

Zhooni-au-gummeeng: Lake Simcoe, Silver waters

Misqua-gummi-zaugau-igun: Red Lake

Suppeewigo-zaugau-igun: Net Lake

Mishi-zaugau-igun: Mille Lacs. A large inland lake

Aupitawi-ipee: Lake Abitibi, half full

Waussawau-gummau: Lake Flambeau, Lake reflecting torch lights

RIVERS: zeepeen

Mushkeegoon zeepih: Muskegon River, Muskeg River

Kun-moozoo zeepih: Kalamazoo River, Moose bone River

Wisconsin zeepih: Wisconsin River

Chippewa-zeepih: Chippewa River

Menominee-zeepih: Menominee River

Mishi-zeepih: Mississippi River, The Great River

Odauwau zeepih: Ottawa River

Aupita-wipee zeepih: **Abitibi River**

Mautau-gummau-zeepih: **Mattagami River**

Ween-ipeeg-zeepih: **Winnipeg River**

Misqua-gummi-zeepih: **Red River**

Gazheeskaudjiwun-zeepih: **Saskatchewan River**

Abeed-waewae-zeepih: **Petawawa River, Coming Sound**

Assinee-bawaun zeepih: **Assiniboine River, Barbeque River**

PLACE NAMES

Akeewaedin **(Keewatin, ON) — The North Wind**
  Akeewae: to go home
  Inoodin: wind

Anim-ipeegoong **(Nipigon, ON) — Along the waterway**
  Anim: along the way
  Nipi: water
  Goong: at the place of
  The term may also mean "pipe stone site" Assinee (stone) and the
  puwaugun (pipe) would certainly yield "nipigon"

Atikokan **(ON) — Caribou bone**
  Addik: caribou
  Kun: a bone

Aum-idjiwunaung **(Sarnia, ON and Port Huron, MI) - At the place where**
  the land slopes

Batchawana — **Place where the waters boil, bubble and well up**
  Ombu: to rise
  Idjiwun: flow, current of water

Baekaudjingum (Pikangikum, ON) — Quiet, placid waters
Baekaudj: placid, peaceful
Gummauh: waters

Bauwiting (Sault Ste. Marie, ON) — At the place of the rapids
Bauwitik: rapids, swift waters
ing: at the place of

Chemong (ON) — A large loon
Kitchi: large, big
Maung: loon

Chicago (IL) — Place of the skunk or leeks
Zhigaug: a skunk
Zhigaugoohnsh: a leek or an onion

Couchiching (ON) — At the edge of a whirlpool or an outlet
Goodjeeng: out, outside
Inidjiiwun: a current

Doodooshuk (Tadoussac, PQ) — Women's breasts
Doodoosh(uk): a breast(s)

Gau-minitik-awaeyauk (Lakehead, ON), Thunder Bay. Many river islands.
Minitik (Ministik - Cree): river islands formed by silt
Waeyauk: of the character of, characterized by

Gau-waubaubigunikauk (White Earth, MN) — White earth or White clay
Gauh: characterized by Waubaubigun or waubigun: clay

Gauh-ziguskawaudjimaekauk (Leech Lake, MN) — The habitat of leeches.
Gauh: habituated, frequented by
Ziguskawaudjimaek: leeches

Gin-ozhae-kauning **(Bay Mills, MI)** — The place of the pike
Ginoo: long, extended
Ozhae: body, torso
Kauning: at, the location of

Kauk-aubeekauh **(Kakabeka, ON)** — A river that falls, flows over a steep
ledge or series of ledges
Kaukau: characterized by
Aubikau: of rock
Aupeekau: water

Kauwautae **(Kawartha)** — Bright waters
Kauwautae: bright, shiny
Gummauk: waters, lake

Kitchi-bee-too-ipeegoong **(Grand Marais, MN)** — An immense pond
Kitchi: immense, large, huge
Beetoo: between
Ipeeg (nipih): water
Ong: place of

Kitchi-Gaugeedjiwung **(Niagara Falls)** — The Great Falls, The Great Flow
Kitchi: great, huge
Geedjiwun: flow over, current

Kitchi-puwaugun **(Cheboygan, MI)** — A large pipe
Kitchi: large
Puwaugun: pipe

Kitchi-winnigum-eeng **(Grand Portage, MI)** — Great or Grand portage
Kitchi: great, grand
Winnigum: portage
Eeng: at the place of

Manitoba (Manitoba) — The land of the manitous; the passage between 2 lakes, a channel, the holy nature of the straits joining 2 bodies of water.

Manitou (many names in Canada and U.S.A.) — A mystery, a spirit, The Creator

Manitou-miniss (Manitoulin Island) — Spirit island
  Manitou: a spirit, mystery
  Miniss: an island

Maniwaukee (Maniwaki, PQ) — A drinking vessel
  Miniquagun: a cup, dipper

Mattawa (ON) — A river flowing into another body of water; the river whose current produces an echo; the beginning
  Mautau: begin, start
  Mauwitau: to collect
  Medawaewae: sound

Mazin-aubik-aung (Painted Rocks, MI) — The painted rocks; rocks with images on them
  Mazin: an image, etching
  Aubik: rock or metal
  Aung: at the place of

Mindemooyaehn (Mindimoya, ON) — An old woman

Mino-meenae (Menominee, WI) — The good seed
  Mino: good, excellent
  Meen: seed, berry

Misheen-maukinauk-oong (Michillimackinac, MI) — The Great Turtle
Mishi: great, immense
Maukinauk: turtle

Mishi-beegwootin-oong (Michipicoten, ON) — The place of the broken,
craggy heights
Mishi: huge, immense
Beegwootin: broken, craggy
Oong: at the place of

Mishi-gummeeng (Michigan, U.S.A.) — The vast body of water
Mishi: immense, vast
Gummeeng: at, by, on, near a large body of water

Mishi-zaugau-igun (Mille Lacs, MN) — The great lake
Mishi: great, large
Zaugau-igun: lake

Mishi-zaugeeng (Mississauga, ON) — The large river outlet
Mishi: great, grand
Zaugeeng: a river outlet

Mishi-zeepi (Mississippi River, USA) — The Great River
Mishi: great, huge, grand
Zeepi: river, stream

Misqua-gummi-zaugau-igun (Red Lake, MN) — Red watered lake
Misqua: red
Inaugummi: the quality of fluid, water
Zaugau-igun: a lake

Misqua-kaung (Muskoka, ON) — The red land, from the autumn crimson
   of trees
   Misqua: red
   Kaung: land, the place where

Mitchi-akeewaedin-oong (Mitchi-geeng) (West Bay, ON) — Directly
   facing the north, the bare north.
   Mitchi: bare, without
   Akee: homeward
   Inoodin: wind

Mitchi-kunneeng (Rama and Atherley, ON) — A fenced-in place referring
   to the weirs in the narrows
   Mitchi: bare, without
   Kun: a bone (bark stripped poles)
   Eeng: at the place of

Mooningwunae-kauning (La Pointe, WI) — The habitat of the lapwing, a
   plover.
   Mooningwunae: a kind of plover
   Kauning: habitat

Mushkeeg (Muskegon, MI) — The Muskeg
   Mushkeg: a muskeg

Mushkeeg-zeebi (Mashki-zeebi) (Bad River, WI) — Erroneously translated
   as "Bad River"; should be "the swampy or muskeg river."
   Mushkeeg: a swamp or muskeg
   Zeepi: a river

Naetau-waush (Nay-tauh-waush, MN) — A great, skilful flyer
   Naetau: skilful, practiced, habitual
   Inaushih: to fly, sail, driven by the wind

Naeyaushee-winnigum-eeng (Cape Croker, ON) — Portage Point
Naeyaush: a point
Winnigum: to portage
Eeng: at the place of

Naudawae-zaugeeng (Nottawassaga, ON) — Mohawk River Mouth
Naudawae: (A Mohawk)
Zaugeeng: a river outlet

Neepissing (Nipissing, ON) — The place of elms, or leaves, or waters.
Nipi: water
Neep: elm
Neebeesh: leaf

Ningo-widjiw (Grand Sable Dunes, MI) — Mountains or hillocks of sand
Nigauwun: fine (white) sand
Widjiw: a mountain

Nipi-meenun (Pembina, MB) — Water berries
Nipi: water
Meenun: berries

Odauwae or Odjauwae (Ottawa, ON) — to trade, barter
Odauwae or odjawae: to exchange, trade
Odauwuhnshk: a kind of bulrush growing in a river, used in the
making of mats and partitions

Ongniarrhra (Niagara) — A bisected bottomland, a bisected riverbed

Ontaraho (Ontario) — The lake?
Iroquoian

Oshawae (Oshawa, ON) — On the other side; to go back and forth
   Auzhiwi: other side, around the corner
   Wae: to make, do, perform

Oshki-naubae (Eskanaba, MI) — New man
   Oshki: new
   Naubae: man, being

Oshki-odaenah (Bayfield, WI) — New town
   Oshki: new
   Odaenah: a town

Pinitauwingausheeng (Penetanguishene, ON) — A sandy peninsula
   Pinitauwun: a kind of sand, gravel
   Ausheeng: a point, peninsula

Pontiak (Pontiac, MI) — An Indian chief who besieged Detroit; now a
   fine automobile
   Boodiwaugun: a fireplace
   Gaboodayaukawauh: an impassible forest

Pusudunnauh (Pasadena, CA) — A valley
   Pussu or pusu: low, lower
   Dunnauh: a land form

Sheesk-audjiwun (Saskatchewan, Canada) — Swift current or river
   Gazheesk (Cree): swift, fast
   Audjiwun: the flow or current of a river

Suppeewigo-zaugau-igun (Net Lake, MI) — Net Lake
   Supp: a net
   Zaugau-igun: a lake

Teemau-gummeeng (Timagami, ON) — Deep Lake, waters
Teemau: deep
Gummeeng: waters

Thorontohen (Toronto, ON) — The reflection of timbers on the waters
Thorontohen: an Iroquoian term

Tigawaeyauminoong (Tahquaemenon, MI) — A shallow river bed
Tigawaeyau: a river bed
Oong: at the place of

Waewae (Wawa, ON): The sound
Waewae: Canada Goose

Waussaukissing (Parry Island, ON) — The place where the trees are
reflected on the waters, a reflection
Wauss: bright, reflecting
Aukissing: set in a certain manner

Wauwiyaeyautinoong (Lake St. Clair, ON & MI) — An oval or round lake
Wauwiyaeyau: round, oval
Itinoong: at the place of

Weenipeego (Lake Winnebago, WI) — A murky, muddied lake
Ween: dirty, unclean
Ipeeyauh: water, fluid

Weenipeegosheeng (Winnipeg, MN) — A murky, muddied lake
Ween: dirty, muddied
Nipti: water

Weequaed-amikoong (Wikwemikong, now Wiky, ON) — Beaver Bay
Weequaed: a bay
Amik: place of beaver
Oong: at the place of

Wisconsin (Wisconsin, U.S.A.) — Either Land of the Muskrat or grasses
Wizhuskoohnse: a little muskrat
Weeshkoohnse: a kind of grass

Zauginaung (Saginaw, MI) — An outlet
Zaugi: an outlet
Inaung: at the place of

Zhaegawaeyaumikoong (Chequamegon, WI) — A long narrow span, an
isthmus, a beaver's home
Zhaegawaeyau: a long blunt span; also a shoal
Amik: a beaver
Oong: place of

Zhauwaenigun (Shawinigan, PQ) — A narrow passageway or south
portage
Zhauwun: South
Winnigum: Portage
Zhaubo: through
Inigun: an instrument

Zheebaunauning (Killarney, ON) — A narrows, a passageway
Zheebau: through
Nauning: at the place of

BIOGRAPHIES

Basil Johnston -
Back in 1968 a grade 5 student, after studying Indians in-depth for
five weeks, asked Basil Johnston, a visitor to the school, "Is that all there
is to Indians, Sir?" Since that time Basil Johnston has written 15 books in
English and 5 in Ojibway to show that there is much more to North
American life than social organization, hunting and fishing, food
preparation, clothing, dwellings and transportation. Among the books
that Basil has written are *Ojibway Heritage, Indian School Days, The
Manitous,* and *Crazy Dave.* In addition he has written numerous articles
that have been published in newspapers, anthologies and periodicals.
But the key to understanding culture is language and to provide this key,
Basil Johnston has developed audio programs on cassette and CD. For
his work, he has received the Order of Ontario and Honourary
Doctorates from the University of Toronto and Laurentian Univeristy.

Polly Keeshig-Tobias, or Zhiibiikweance -
Little river woman, a name given to her by her grandfather, refers to her
"gift of gab." Growing up, she was surround by artists, actors, poets,
and storytellers in Toronto's Aboriginal community. Ojiwbay and Leni
Lanaape, Turtle Cane, she is the middle of three sisters, her mother
lovingly refers to as "Corn, Bean and Squash." She has returned home, to
her reserve, Neyaashiinigaamiing, Cape Croker, where she is learning to
speak Ojibway, and spending time with her family. She has illustrated
four books, and plans on many more.

Ken Syrette -
An Anishinaubae member of the Batchewana First Nation, in Ontario,
his art has been described as lyrical and joyful, often humorous, and
always colourful. Ken lives and works out of Toronto, Ontario.

CPSIA information can be obtained
at www.ICGtesting.com
Printed in the USA
LVHW020007210721
693202LV00015B/1486